The Faber Book of Blue Verse

The Faber Book of BLUE VERSE

Edited by John Whitworth

faber and faber

LONDON · BOSTON

First published in 1990
by Faber and Faber Limited
3 Queen Square London WC1N 3AU

Photoset by Wilmaset Birkenhead Wirral
Printed in England by
Clays Ltd, St Ives plc

This collection © John Whitworth, 1990

A CIP record for this book
is available from the British Library

ISBN 0-571-14095-5

You often say my work is coarse. It's true;
But then it must be so – it deals with you.

MARTIAL
translated by J. A. Potts

Contents

CONTENTS

[viii]

ON THE ROCKS

IMAGINE

WICKED WORDS

THAT HOUSE OF PLEASURE

Eskimo Nell

When men grow old and their balls grow cold,
   And the end of their tool turns blue,
Far from that life of Yukon strife
   They'll tell a tale that's true.

So bring me a seat, and buy me a drink,
   And a tale to you I'll tell
Of Deadeye Dick and Mexico Pete
   And a whore named Eskimo Nell.

When Mexico Pete and Deadeye Dick
   Set out in search of fun,
It's Deadeye Dick who wields the prick
   And Mexico Pete the gun.

When Deadeye Dick and the greaser runt
   Were sore distressed and sad
'Twas mostly cunt that bore the brunt
   Though shootings weren't so bad.

When Deadeye Dick and Mexico Pete
   Went down to Deadman's Creek,
They'd had no luck, in the way of fuck,
   For well nigh half a week,

Bar a moose or two or a caribou
   And a bison cow or so,
But Deadeye Dick was the king of pricks
   And he found such fucking slow.

So Deadeye Dick and Mexico Pete
   Set out for the Rio Grande;
Deadeye Dick with swinging prick,
   And Pete with gun in hand.

And thus they blazed their randy trail,
   And none their fire withstood,
And many a bride who was hubby's pride
   Knew pregnant widowhood.

They hit the bank of the Rio Grande
   At the height of blazing noon
To slake their thirst and do their worst
   They sought Red Kate's Saloon.

And as they strode into the bar
   Both prick and gun flashed free:
'According to sex you drunken wrecks,
   You drinks or fucks with me.'

They knew the fame of our heroes' name
   From the Horn to Panama
So with little worse than a muttered curse
   Those dagos lined the bar.

The women knew his playful ways
   Way down on the Rio Grande
So forty whores tore down their drawers
   At Deadeye Dick's command.

They saw the fingers of Mexico Pete
   Touching his pistol grip,
They didn't waste, in frantic haste
   Those whores began to strip.

Deadeye Dick was breathing hard
   With noisy snarls and grunts
As forty arses came into view
   To say nothing of forty cunts.

Now forty arses and forty cunts
   You'll find, if you use your wits,
And if you're quick at arithmetic,
   Signifies eighty tits.

[4]

Now eighty tits is a goodly sight
  To a man with a mighty stand;
It may be rare in Berkeley Square
  But not on the Rio Grande.

Now to test his wind, he'd had a grind
  The previous Saturday night,
And this he'd done to show his fun
  And whet his appetite.

His phallic limb was in fighting trim
  So he backed and took a run,
He took a jump at the nearest rump
  And scored a hole in one.

He bore her to the sandy floor,
  And fairly fucked her fine,
But though she grinned, it put the wind
  Up the other thirty-nine.

For when Deadeye Dick performs the trick
  There's scarcely time to spare,
For with speed and strength, on top of length
  He fairly singes hair.

Now Deadeye Dick he fucks 'em quick,
  And has cast the first aside.
He made a dart at the second tart,
  When the swing doors opened wide.

Then entered in that hall of sin,
  Into that house of hell,
A lusty maid, no whit afraid,
  Her name – was Eskimo Nell.

Now Deadeye Dick had got his prick
  Well into number two
When Eskimo Nell let out a yell
  And called to him 'Hi you!'

He gave a flick of his muscular prick
  And the whore flew over his head,
He turned about with a snarl and a shout
  And his face and his knob were red.

Eskimo Nell she stood it well
  As she looked between his eyes.
She glanced with scorn upon his horn
  Steaming between his thighs.

She stubbed out the butt of her cigarette
  On the end of his gleaming knob,
And so utterly beat was Mexico Pete
  That he quite forgot his job.

It was Eskimo Nell who was first to speak,
  In accents clear and cool,
'You cuntstruck shrimp of a Yankee pimp
  Do you call that thing a tool?

And if this here town can't take it down,'
  She sneered at the cowering whores,
'Here's a cunt that can do the stunt:
  Eskimo Nell, for yours!'

She removed her garments one by one
  With an air of conscious pride
Till there she stood in her womanhood
  And they saw the Great Divide.

'Tis fair to state 'twas not so great
  Though its strength lay well within
And a better word, that's often heard,
  Would not be *cunt* but *quim*.

She laid her down on the table-top
  Whereon was set a glass,
With a flick of her tits she ground it to bits
  Between the cheeks of her arse.

[6]

She bent her knees with supple ease
  And spread them wide apart,
And with smiling nods to the randy sods
  She gave him the cue to start.

But Deadeye Dick, he knew a trick
  Or two, and he took his time,
For a miss like this was perfect bliss
  So he played in a pantomime.

He flicked his foreskin up and down
  He made his balls inflate
Until they resembled two granite knobs
  Upon a garden gate.

He winked his arsehole in and out
  And his balls increased in size;
His mighty prick grew twice as thick
  And nearly reached his eyes.

He polished it well with alcohol,
  To get it steaming hot,
And to finish the job, he peppered the knob
  With the cayenne pepper pot.

He didn't back and take a run,
  Or make a flying leap,
He didn't swoop, but made a stoop,
  And a steady forward creep.

With peering eyes he took a sight
  Along that fearsome tool,
And the long slow glide as it slid inside
  Was calculating – cool.

Now you all have seen the pistons gleam
  On the mighty CPR
With the driving force of a thousand horse
  So you know what pistons are.

Or you think you do, if you've yet to view
   The power that drives the prick,
Or the work that's done on a non-stop run,
   By a man like Deadeye Dick.

None but a fool would challenge his tool,
   No thinking man would doubt
For his fame increased as the Great High Priest
   Of the ceaseless in-and-out.

But Eskimo Nell was an infidel
   And equalled a whole harem,
With the strength of ten in her abdomen,
   And a Rock of Ages' beam.

Amidships she could stand a rush
   Like the flush of a water closet,
So she gripped his cock like the Chatwood lock
   Of the National Safe Deposit.

But Deadeye Dick would not come quick,
   He meant to conserve his powers,
When in the mind he'd grind and grind
   For more than a couple of hours.

She lay a while with a subtle smile
   And then her grip grew keener,
And with a sigh she sucked him dry
   With the ease of a vacuum cleaner.

She did this feat in a way so neat
   As to set at grand defiance
The primary cause of the basic laws
   That govern all sexual science.

She simply rode that phallic tool,
   That for years had stood the test,
And accepted rules of the ancient schools
   In a second or two went west!

[8]

And now my friend we near the end
 Of this copulative epic
For the effect on Dick was so sudden and quick
 'Twas akin to an anaesthetic.

He slid to the floor, and knew no more,
 His passion extinct and dead.
He didn't shout as his tool slipped out
 'Though 'tis said she'd stripped the thread.

Then Mexico Pete, he rose to his feet
 To avenge his friend's affront
And his tough-nosed Colt with a savage jolt
 He rammed right up her cunt.

He shoved it hard to the trigger guard
 And fired it twice times three
But to his surprise she closed her eyes
 And squealed in ecstasy.

As she rose to her feet, she looked so sweet
 'Bully!' she cried, 'for you;
Though I might have guessed it's about the best
 That you poor sods could do.'

When next, my friends, you two intend
 To sally forth for fun,
Get Deadeye Dick a sugar stick
 And buy yourself a bun.

For I'm away to the frozen North,
 Where pricks are big and strong,
Back to the land of the frozen stand
 Where the nights are six months long.

When you stick it in it's as hard as sin,
 In a land where spunk is spunk,
Not a trickling steam of lukewarm cream
 But a solid frozen chunk.

Back to the land where they understand
  What it means to copulate,
Where even the dead lie two in a bed
  And the children masturbate.

Back once more to the sins of men,
  To the Land of the Midnight Sun,
I go to spend a worthy end
  For the north is calling '*Come!*'

ANON.

And I Lounged and Lay on Their Beds

When I went to that house of pleasure
I didn't stay in the front rooms where they celebrate,
with some decorum, the accepted modes of love.

I went into the secret rooms
and lounged and lay on their beds.

I went into the secret rooms
considered shameful even to name.
But not shameful to me – because if they were,
what kind of poet, what kind of artist would I be?
I'd rather be an ascetic. That would be more in keeping,
much more in keeping with my poetry,
than for me to find pleasure in the commonplace rooms.

C. P. CAVAFY
translated by Edmund Keeley and Philip Sherrard

Variations and Excerpts

'Ballocky Bill the Sailor'

Who's that crepitating with his knuckledusters on my
    portico?
Who's the man aggressifying his digits on my doorbox?
Who is the person terrifying the nightwood with his fistfuls?
    cried the beauteous young virgin
    (called the youthful female winner of Beauty Prizes)
    (enunciated the scarcely mature attractive lady)

It is only I from the mighty recesses of Ocean, cried William
    the Mightily-testiculated Mariner
(At your service, my Lady, from the scaly squadrons' lair,
    intimated Guglielmo, the Man of Parts, the Seafarer)
(Here I am after a rough crossing, said Willie the Well-
    endowed Water-wanderer)

I will descend then and admit you
I'll go below and allow you up
'Tis I will sink that you may rise
    cried the freshly formed teenage trollop
    (lisped her lovely under-twenty Ladyship)
    (opined the new slick chick)

I am ancient and rugose and a stranger to the bath and yet
    vigorous, yelled Will the Well-hung Matelot
(Many summers have I seen, my skin is no longer smooth,
    nor is it sanitate, but I maintain my strength, cracked
    Billy the Ballsy Bo'sun)
(No more am I youthful, my manners are crude, I am not
    well-washed, but I am nevertheless full of energy,
    explained Guillaume the Big-balled Waterman) . . .

GAVIN EWART

The Gallant Irish Yeoman

When the Irish regiments returned in June 1900 from a series of victorious campaigns for the British Army in the Boer War, this ode appeared in *Irish Society*, a kind of *Tatler* of the time and place. The magazine sold out within the hour. If you are acrostically minded you will soon see why. The anonymous author was soon revealed as Gogarty, a leading contributor to Arthur Griffith's paper *Sinn Fein*.

The Gallant Irish Yeoman
Home from the wars has come,
Each victory gained o'er foeman,
Why should our bards be dumb.

How shall we sing their praises
Or glory in their deeds,
Renowned their worth amazes,
Empire their prowess needs.

So to Old Ireland's hearts and homes
We welcome now our own brave boys
In cot and hall; 'neath lordly domes
Love's heroes share once more our joys.

Love is the Lord of all just now,
Be he the husband, lover, son,
Each dauntless soul recalls the vow
By which not fame, but love was won.

United now in fond embrace
Salute with joy each well-loved face.
Yeoman, in women's hearts you hold the place.

                    OLIVER ST JOHN GOGARTY

Housewife Hooker

Just before she gets the kids from school
In Bos en Lommer, Erica van Hool
Sucks some fat and total stranger's tool.

'Hoeveel kost het?' he says, zipping his pants.
She clears her throat, and tells him. No romance;
Just old Dutch trade, manipulating chance

Into design, the way Rembrandt van Rijn
Did with paint till 1669.
He nods, and leaves, the groot becoming klein

Inside his Y-fronts. In the Dormobile
She hums Corelli absent-mindedly.
Is life a dream? And is the dream for real?
Before her husband homes, she'll lay his tea

Decorously, and change the window's flowers.
The girl does cello lessons in her room.
The boy just eats an apple. Mankind's powers
She hopes will one day make the desert bloom.

Betweentimes, she donates to charity,
And goes to church with regularity,
And works from home – at least, till half-past three.

PAUL GROVES

We're at the Bath-house

We're at the bath-house. I
Chat the big, cocky boys up. Why?
What is it that they do?
They bugger nosy sods like you.

MARTIAL
translated by Fergus Pickering

Lucky Spence's Last Advice

Three times the carline grain'd and rifted,
Then frae the cod her pow she lifted,
In bawdy policy well gifted,
    When she now fan
That death nae longer wad be shifted,
    She thus began:

'My loving lasses, I maun leave ye;
But dinna wi' your greeting grieve me,
Nor wi your draunts and droning deave me,
    But bring's a gill;
For faith, my bairns, ye may believe me,
    'Tis 'gainst my will.

'O black-ey'd Bess, and mim-mou'd Meg,
O'er good to work, or yet to beg,
Lay sunkets up for a sair leg;
    For when ye fail,
Ye'r face will not be worth a feg,
    Nor yet ye'r tail.

'Whane'er ye meet a fool that's fou,
That ye're a maiden gar him trow,
Seem nice, but stick to him like glue
    And when set down,
Drive at the jango till he spew,
    Syne he'll sleep sown.

'When he's asleep, then dive and catch
His ready cash, his rings, or watch;

carline old woman
cod bolster
sunkets provisions
feg fig
gar him trow make him believe

And gin he likes to light his match
    At your spunk-box,
Ne'er stand to let the fumbling wretch
    E'en take the pox.

'Cleek a' ye can by hook or crook,
Rype ilka pouch frae nook to nook;
Be sure to truff his pocket-book —
    Saxty pounds Scots
Is nae deaf nits; in little bouk
    Lie great bank notes.

'To get amends of whingeing fools
That's frighted for repenting-stools,
Wha often whan their metal cools
    Turn sweer to pay;
Gar the kirk-boxie hale the dools
    Anither day.

'But dawt red-coats, and let them scoup
Free for the fou of cutty stoup;
To gee them up, ye needna hope
    E'er to do weel;
They'll rive ye'r brats, and kick your doup,
    And play the deel.

'There's ae sair cross attends the craft,
That curst correction-house, where aft
Wild hangy's tawse ye'er riggings saft

truff search
Is nae deaf nits Is not nothing
sweer reluctant
Gar the kirk-boxie hale the dools   let the church-box win the game
dawt pet
scoup fuck
cutty stoup small beer
rive ye'r brats, and kick your doup   tear your knickers, and kick your arse
hangy's tawse the hangman's whip
riggings saft backside

Makes black and blae,
Enough to put a body daft;
But what'll ye say?

'Nane gaithers gear withouten care,
Ilk pleasure has of pain a share;
Suppose then they should tirle ye bare,
And gar ye sike,
E'en learn to thole; 'tis very fair,
Ye're nibour-like.

'Forby, my loves, count upo' losses,
Ye'r milk-white teeth, and cheeks like roses,
Whan jet-black hair and brigs of noses
Fa' doon wi' dads,
To keep your hearts up 'neath sic crosses,
Set up for bawds.

'Wi' well-creeshed loofs I hae been canty.
Whan e'er the lads wad fain ha'e faun t'ye,
To try the auld game taunty-raunty,
Like coosers keen,
They took advice of me, your aunty,
If ye were clean.

'Then up I took my siller ca',
And whistl'd benn, whiles ane whiles twa;
Roun'd in his lug that there was a
Poor country Kate,
As halesome as the well of Spa,
But unca blate.

gar ye sike make you weep
thole endure
dads lumps
well-creeshed loofs well-greased palms
coosers stallions
siller ca' silver whistle
unca blate very shy

'Sae when e'er company came in,
And were upon a merry pin,
I slade awa' wi' little din
        And muckle mense,
Lest conscience judge, it was a' ane
        To Lucky Spence.

'My bennison come on good doers
Wha spend their cash on bawds and whores;
May they ne'er want the wale of cures
        For a sair snout;
Foul fa' the quacks wha that fire smoors,
        And puts nae out.

'My malison light ilka day
On them that drink and dinna pay,
But tak' a snack and run away;
        May't be their hap
Never to want a gonorrhoea
        Or rotten clap.

'Lass, gi'e us in anither gill.
A mutchken, jo, let's tak' our fill;
Let Death syne registrate his bill
        Whan I want sense,
I'll slip awa' wi' better will' –
        Quo' Lucky Spence.

ALLAN RAMSAY

merry pin merry mood
mense discretion
Foul fa' a curse on
smoors smothers

Two Young Men, 23 to 24 Years Old

He'd been sitting in the café since ten-thirty
expecting him to turn up any minute.
Midnight had gone, and he was still waiting for him.
It was now after one-thirty, and the café was almost
    deserted.
He'd grown tired of reading newspapers
mechanically. Of his three lonely shillings
only one was left: waiting that long,
he'd spent the others on coffees and brandy.
And he'd smoked all his cigarettes.
So much waiting had worn him out.
Because alone like that for so many hours,
he'd also begun to have disturbing thoughts
about the immoral life he was living.

But when he saw his friend come in —
weariness, boredom, thought all disappeared at once.

His friend brought unexpected news.
He'd won sixty pounds playing cards.

Their good looks, their exquisite youthfulness,
the sensitive love they shared
were refreshed, livened, invigorated
by the sixty pounds from the card table.

Now all joy and vitality, feeling and charm,
they went — not to the homes of their respectable families
(where they were no longer wanted anyway) —
they went to a familiar and very special
house of debauchery, and they asked for a bedroom
and expensive drinks, and they drank again.

And when the expensive drinks were finished
and it was close to four in the morning,
happy, they gave themselves to love.

C. P. CAVAFY
translated by Edmund Keeley and Philip Sherrard

Diamond Lily

Oh, my name is Diamond Lily.
I'm a whore in Piccadilly
And my father runs a brothel in the Strand
My brother sells his arsehole
To the Guards at Windsor Castle.
We're the finest fucking family in the land.

ANON.

Columbiad: Two Stanzos

The Ladies of King Bolo's Court
Were called 'The Broadway Benders',
And likewise called 'The Fore and Aft'
Or else 'The Double Enders'.
Columbo took a single look
And hitched up his suspenders.
'Come on, my merry men' said he:
'*These* look like old offenders.'

King Bolo's Royal Body Guard
Were called 'The Jersey Lilies' –
A bold and bestial set of blacks
Undaunted by syphilis.
They wore the national uniform
Of a garland of verbenas
And a pair of big black hairy balls
And a big black knotty penis.

T. S. ELIOT

There was a young girl of Siberia

There was a young girl of Siberia
Who had such a tempting posterior
That the Lapps and the Finns
Kept inventing new sins
As the recognized types were too stereo –

T. S. ELIOT

'Twas Christmas on the Spanish Main

'Twas Christmas on the Spanish Main,
The wind it up and blew hard;
The vessel gave an awful lurch
And heeled 'way down to leeward.
The Chaplain was so very scared
His breeches he manured;
And Columbo slid along the deck
And raped the smoke-room steward.

T. S. ELIOT

Male Order

Today it's schoolgirl shots. Janie
(16) starts in navy gymslip,
Daz-white blouse – a bit
tight now, of course, but

that's a bonus for the punters –
and regulation navy-blue knickers,
topped up by sheer stockings
and a neat little garter belt.

Shirl mans the Nikon in her attic-cum-
studio *(away from the nosy parkers).*
Janie strips quite prettily
and makes good use of a hockey stick.

Mum models for the 'Older Women' sets
and helps Shirl out with the business side.
Janie's quite taken to it
and confesses that 'open-leg' shots

really make me feel fruity.
This, of course, comes in handy
for 'self' shots. *(You can always tell,*
says Shirl, *when they're simulated.)*

For stronger material – F/F, F/M –
plump Mandy, big Jim and Roger oblige.
We don't do videos, says Shirl, *so
we don't need props like shaving foam.*

*Besides, I don't like conning the punters.
Roger's still a bit quick when Janie's
in the belt and white seamed-stockings.
Jim does the 'three-sets' with Janie and Mandy.*

The girls get through an awful lot of stockings.
But the pastel shades they do now
come out so well on the colour sets.
Thank God for Dorothy Perkins.

After 'Schoolgirl Sex', 'Mixed Doubles'
and 'French Oral' are the most popular.
For 'Girls Only', *Mandy was a great find.*
39D-cup. A bit that way inclined,

which helps. Mum says: *I think it's all*
worth it for those little extras in life.
And it'll set Janie and Roger up nicely
for when they get married.

ROBERT MAITRE

The Ruined Maid

'O 'Melia, my dear, this does everything crown!
Who could have supposed I should meet you in Town?
And whence such fair garments, such prosperi-ty?' –
'O didn't you know I'd been ruined?' said she.

– 'You left us in tatters, without shoes or socks,
Tired of digging potatoes, and spudding up docks;
And now you've gay bracelets and bright feathers three!' –
'Yes: that's how we dress when we're ruined,' said she.

– 'At home in the barton you said "thee" and "thou",
And "thik oon", and "theäs oon", and "t'other"; but now
Your talking quite fits 'ee for high compa-ny!' –
'Some polish is gained with one's ruin,' said she.

– 'Your hands were like paws then, your face blue and
    bleak
But now I'm bewitched by your delicate cheek,
And your little gloves fit as on any la-dy!' –
'We never do work when we're ruined,' said she.

– 'You used to call home-life a hag-ridden dream,
And you'd sigh, and you'd sock; but at present you seem
To know not of megrims or melancho-ly!' –
'True. One's pretty lively when ruined,' said she.

– 'I wish I had feathers, a fine sweeping gown,
And a delicate face, and could strut about Town!' –
'My dear – a raw country girl, such as you be,
Cannot quite expect that. You ain't ruined,' said she.

THOMAS HARDY

THE DAILY ROUND

Aberdarcy: the Chaucer Road

5.40. The Bay View. After the office,
Evans drops in for a quick glass of stout,
Then, by the fruit-machine, runs into Haydn,
Who's marrying the kid he's nuts about.

Of course, he won't pretend it's all been easy:
The wife's three-quarters off her bloody head,
And Gwyneth being younger than their youngest
Leaves certain snags still to be combated.

Oh, no gainsaying that she's quite a handful;
No, not bad-tempered, man, just a bit wild.
He likes a girl to show a touch of spirit;
It's all the better when you're reconciled.

And then, dear dear, what dizzy peaks of passion!
Not only sex, but mind and spirit too,
Like in that thing Prof Hughes took with the Honours:
That's right, *The Rainbow* – well, it's all come true.

6.10. The Humber. Evans starts reflecting
How much in life he's never going to know:
All it must mean to really love a woman.
He pulls up sharp outside a bungalow.

6.30. Balls to where. In like a whippet;
A fearsome thrash with Mrs No-holds-barred
(Whose husband's in his surgery till 7);
Back at the wheel 6.50, breathing hard.

7.10. 'Braich-y-Pwll'. – 'Hallo now, Megan.
No worse than usual, love. You been all right?
Well, this looks good. And there's a lot on later;
Don't think I'll bother with the club tonight.'

Nice bit of haddock with poached egg, Dundee cake.
Buckets of tea, then a light ale or two,
And 'Gunsmoke', 'Danger Man', the Late Night Movie –
Who's doing better, then? What about you?

KINGSLEY AMIS

The Miller's Tale

Whilom ther was dwellynge at Oxenford
A riche gnof, that gestes heeld to bord,
And of his craft he was a carpenter.
With hym ther was dwellynge a povre scoler,
Hadde lerned art, but al his fantasye
Was turned for to lerne astrologye,
And koude a certeyn of conclusiouns,
To demen by interrogaciouns,
If that men asked hym in certein houres
Whan that men sholde have droghte or elles shoures,
Or if men asked hym what sholde bifalle
Of every thyng; I may nat rekene hem alle.
This clerk was cleped hende Nicholas.
Of deerne love he koude and of solas;
And therto he was sleigh and ful privee,
And lyk a mayden meke for to see.
A chambre hadde he in that hostelrye
Allone, withouten any compaignye,
Ful fetisly ydight with herbes swoote;
And he hymself as sweete as is the roote
Of lycorys, or any cetewale.
His Almageste, and bookes grete and smale,
His astrelabie, longynge for his art,
His augrym stones layen faire apart,

gnof oaf
gestes guests
koude a certeyn of conclusiouns knew some propositions
cleped hende called clever
Of deerne love he koude and of solas he knew about secret love and pleasure
fetisly ydight pleasantly decorated
swoote sweet
cetewale ginger
Almageste an astrological treatise
astrelabie an astrological instrument
longynge for belonging to
augrym stones counting stones

On shelves couched at his beddes heed;
His presse ycovered with a faldyng reed;
And al above ther lay a gay sautrie,
On which he made a-nyghtes melodie
So swetely that al the chambre rong;
And *Angelus ad virginem* he song;
And after that he song the kynges noote.
Ful often blessed was his myrie throte.
And thus this sweete clerk his tyme spente
After his freendes fyndyng and his rente.

 This carpenter hadde wedded newe a wyf,
Which that he lovede moore than his lyf;
Of eighteteene yeer she was of age.
Jalous he was, and heeld hire narwe in cage,
For she was wylde and yong, and he was old,
An demed hymself been lik a cokewold.
He knew nat Catoun, for his wit was rude,
That bad man sholde wedde his simylitude.
Men sholde wedden after hire estaat,
For youthe and elde is often at debaat.
But sith that he was fallen in the snare,
He moste endure, as oother folk, his care.

 Fair was this yonge wyf, and therwithal
As any wesele hir body gent and smal.
A ceynt she werede, barred al of silk,
A barmclooth eek as whit as morne milk
Upon hir lendes, ful of many a goore.
Whit was hir smok, and broyden al bifoore
And eek bihynde, on hir coler aboute,

faldyng reed red cloth
sautrie psaltery
After his freendes fyndyng and his rente living off his friends' money
ceynt girdle
barmclooth apron
lendes loins
ful of many a goore made up of many pieces
broyden embroidered

[34]

Of col-blak silk, withinne and eek withoute.
The tapes of hir white voluper
Were of the same suyte of hir coler;
Hir filet brood of silk, and set ful hye.
And sikerly she hadde a likerous yë;
Ful smale ypulled were hire browes two,
And tho were bent and blake as any sloo.
She was ful moore blisful on to see
Than is the newe pere-jonette tree,
And softer than the wolle is of a wether.
And by hir girdel heeng a purs of lether,
Tasseled with silk, and perled with latoun.
In al this world, to seken up and doun,
There nys no man so wys that koude thenche
So gay a popelote or swich a wenche.
Ful brighter was the shynyng of hir hewe
Than in the Tour the noble yforged newe.
But of hir song, it was as loude and yerne
As any swalwe sittynge on a berne.
Therto she koude skippe and make game,
As any kyde or calf folwynge his dame.
Hir mouth was sweete as bragot or the meeth,
Or hoord of apples leyd in hey or heeth.
Wynsynge she was as is a joly colt,
Long as a mast, and upright as a bolt.
A brooch she baar upon hir lowe coler,

voluper bonnet
same suyte of hir coler same material as her collar
sloo sloe
pere-jonette tree kind of pear-tree
wolle wool
perled with latoun studded with brass
popelote darling
Tour Tower (the mint)
noble gold coin
berne barn
bragot or the meeth honey-and-ale or mead
wynsynge skittish

As brood as is the boos of a bokeler.
Hir shoes were laced on hir legges hye.
She was a prymerole, a piggesnye,
For any lord to leggen in his bedde,
Or yet for any good yeman to wedde.
   Now, sire, and eft, sire, so bifel the cas,
That on a day this hende Nicholas
Fil with this yonge wyf to rage and pleye,
Whil that hir housbonde was at Oseneye,
As clerkes ben ful subtile and ful queynte;
And prively he caughte hire by the queynte,
And seyde, 'Ywis, but if ich have my wille,
For deerne love of thee, lemman, I spille.'
And heeld hire harde by the haunche-bones,
And seyde, 'Lemman, love me al atones,
Or I wol dyen, also God me save!'
And she sproong as a colt dooth in the trave,
And with hir heed she wryed faste awey,
And seyde, 'I wol nat kisse thee, by my fey!
Why, lat be,' quod she, 'lat be, Nicholas,
Or I wol crie, "out, harrow" and "allas"!
Do wey youre handes, for youre curteisye!'
   This Nicholas gan mercy for to crye,
And spak so faire, and profred him so faste,
That she hir love hym graunted atte laste,
And swoor hir ooth, by seint Thomas of Kent,
That she wol been at his comandement,
Whan that she may hir leyser wel espie.

boos of a bokeler boss of a shield
prymerole primrose
piggesnye a little flower (cuckoo flower)
pleye dally
queynte cunning
deerne secret
atones at once
trave enclosure
harrow help!
leyser opportunity

'Myn housbonde is so ful of jalousie
That but ye wayte wel and been privee,
I woot right wel I nam but deed,' quod she.
'Ye moste been ful deerne, as in this cas.'
    'Nay, therof care thee noght,' quod Nicholas.
'A clerk hadde litherly biset his whyle,
But if he koude a carpenter bigyle.'
And thus they been accorded and ysworn
To wayte a tyme, as I have told biforn.

    Whan Nicholas had doon thus everideel,
And thakked hire aboute the lendes weel,
He kist hire sweete and taketh his sawtrie,
And pleyeth faste, and maketh melodie.

    Thanne fil it thus, that to the paryssh chirche,
Cristes owene werkes for to wirche,
This goode wyf wente on an haliday.
Hir forheed shoon as bright as any day,
So was it wasshen whan she leet hir werk.
Now was ther of that chirche a parissh clerk,
The which that was ycleped Absolon.
Crul was his heer, and as the gold it shoon,
And strouted as a fanne large and brode;
Ful streight and evene lay his joly shode.
His rode was reed, his eyen greye as goos.
With Poules wyndow corven on his shoos,
In hoses rede he wente fetisly.
Yclad he was ful smal and proprely
Al in a kirtel of a lyght waget;

litherly biset his whyle wasted his time
thakked hire aboute the lendes weel stroked her bottom
sawtrie psaltery
crul curly
strouted spead out
shode hair-parting
rode complexion
Poules wyndow Paul's window
fetisly neatly
waget blue

[37]

Ful faire and thikke been the poyntes set.
And therupon he hadde a gay surplys
As whit as is the blosme upon the rys.
A myrie child he was, so God me save.
Wel koude he laten blood and clippe and shave,
And maken a chartre of lond or acquitaunce.
In twenty manere koude he trippe and daunce
After the scole of Oxenforde tho,
And with his legges casten to and fro,
And pleyen songes on a smal rubible;
Therto he song som tyme a loud quynyble;
And as wel koude he pleye on a giterne.
In al the toun nas brewhous ne taverne
That he ne visited with his solas,
Ther any gaylard tappestere was.
But sooth to seyn, he was somdeel squaymous
Of fartyng, and of speche daungerous.

   This Absolon, that jolif was and gay,
Gooth with a sencer on the haliday,
Sensynge the wyves of the parisshe faste;
And many a lovely look on hem he caste,
And namely on this carpenteris wyf.
To looke on hire hym thoughte a myrie lyf,
She was so propre and sweete and likerous.
I dar wel seyn, if she hadde been a mous,
And he a cat, he wolde hire hente anon.
This parissh clerk, this joly Absolon,
Hath in his herte swich a love-longynge
That of no wyf took he noon offrynge;

laten blood and clippe let blood and cut hair
maken a chartre draw up legal deeds
rubible rebec (an early fiddle)
quynyble falsetto
gaylard tappestere lively barmaid
squaymous squeamish
daungerous fastidious
hente caught

For curteisie, he seyde, he wolde noon.
    The moone, whan it was nyght, ful brighte shoon,
And Absolon his gyterne hath ytake,
For paramours he thoghte for to wake.
And forth he gooth, jolif and amorous,
Til he cam to the carpenteres hous
A litel after cokkes hadde ycrowe,
And dressed hym up by a shot-wyndowe
That was upon the carpenteris wal.
He syngeth in his voys gentil and smal,
'Now, deere lady, if thy wille be,
I praye yow that ye wole rewe on me,'
Ful wel acordaunt to his gyternynge.
This carpenter awook, and herde him synge,
And spak unto his wyf, and seyde anon,
'What! Alison! herestow nat Absolon,
That chaunteth thus under oure boures wal?'
And she answerde hir housbonde therwithal,
'Yis, God woot, John, I heere it every deel.'
    This passeth forth; what wol ye bet than weel?
Fro day to day this joly Absolon
So woweth hire that hym is wo bigon.
He waketh al the nyght and al the day;
He kembeth his lokkes brode, and made hym gay;
He woweth hire by meenes and brocage,
And swoor he wolde been hir owene page;
He syngeth, brokkynge as a nyghtyngale;
He sente hire pyment, meeth, and spiced ale,
And wafres, pipyng hoot out of the gleede;
And, for she was of towne, he profred meede.

shot-wyndowe a casement window
rewe on me pity me
meenes and brocage go-betweens
brokkynge trilling
pyment, meeth honeyed wine, mead
wafres waffles
gleede fire

For som folk wol ben wonnen for richesse,
And somme for strokes, and somme for gentillesse.
    Somtyme, to shewe his lightnesse and maistrye,
He pleyeth Herodes upon a scaffold hye.
But what availleth hym as in this cas?
She loveth so this hende Nicholas
That Absolon may blowe the bukkes horn;
He ne hadde for his labour but a scorn.
And thus she maketh Absolon hire ape,
And al his ernest turneth til a jape.
Ful sooth is this proverbe, it is no lye,
Men seyn right thus, 'Alwey the nye slye
Maketh the ferre leeve to be looth.'
For though that Absolon be wood or wrooth,
By cause that he fer was from hire sighte,
This nye Nicholas stood in his lighte.
    Now bere thee wel, thou hende Nicholas,
For Absolon may waille and synge 'allas'.
And so bifel it on a Saterday,
This carpenter was goon til Osenay;
And hende Nicholas and Alisoun
Acorded been to this conclusioun,
That Nicholas shal shapen hym a wyle
This sely jalous housbonde to bigyle;
And if so be the game wente aright,
She sholde slepen in his arm al nyght,
For this was his desir and hire also.
And right anon, withouten wordes mo,
This Nicholas no lenger wolde tarie,
But dooth ful softe unto his chambre carie
Bothe mete and drynke for a day or tweye,
And to hire housbonde bad hire for to seye,

blowe the bukkes horn whistle for it
nye slye nearby sly one
ferre leeve faraway lover

If that he axed after Nicholas,
She sholde seye she nyste where he was,
Of al that day she saugh hym nat with yë;
She trowed that he was in maladye,
For for no cry hir mayde koude hym calle,
He nolde answere for thyng that myghte falle.
　This passeth forth al thilke Saterday,
That Nicholas stille in his chambre lay,
And eet and sleep, or dide what hym leste,
Til Sonday, that the sonne gooth to reste.
This sely carpenter hath greet merveyle
Of Nicholas, or what thyng myghte hym eyle,
And seyde, 'I am adrad, by Seint Thomas,
It stondeth nat aright with Nicholas.
God shilde that he deyde sodeynly!
This world is now ful tikel, sikerly.
I saugh to-day a cors yborn to chirche
That now, on Monday last, I saugh hym wirche.
　'Go up,' quod he unto his knave anoon,
'Clepe at his dore, or knokke with a stoon.
Looke how it is, and tel me boldely.'
　This knave gooth hym up ful sturdily,
And at the chambre dore whil that he stood,
He cride and knokked as that he were wood,
'What! how! what do ye, maister Nicholay?
How may ye slepen al the longe day?'
　But al for noght, he herde nat a word.
An hole he foond, ful lowe upon a bord,
Ther as the cat was wont in for to crepe,
And at that hole he looked in ful depe,
And at the laste he hadde of hym a sighte.
This Nicholas sat evere capyng uprighte,

nyste did not know
tikel uncertain
knave servant
wood mad

As he had kiked on the newe moone.
Adoun he gooth, and tolde his maister soone
In what array he saugh this ilke man.
   This carpenter to blessen hym bigan,
And seyde, 'Help us, seinte Frydeswyde!
A man woot litel what hym shal bityde.
This man is falle, with his astromye,
In som woodnesse or in som agonye.
I thoghte ay wel how that it sholde be!
Men sholde nat knowe of Goddes pryvetee.
Ye, blessed be alwey a lewed man
That noght but oonly his bileve kan!
So ferde another clerk with astromye;
He walked in the feeldes, for to prye
Upon the sterres, what ther sholde bifalle,
Til he was in a marle-pit yfalle;
He saugh nat that. But yet, by seint Thomas,
Me reweth soore of hende Nicholas.
He shal be rated of his studiyng,
If that I may, by Jhesus, hevene kyng!
Get me a staf, that I may underspore,
Whil that thou, Robyn, hevest up the dore.
He shal out of his studiyng, as I gesse' –
And to the chambre dore he gan hym dresse.
His knave was a strong carl for the nones,
And by the haspe he haaf it of atones;
Into the floor the dore fil anon.
This Nicholas sat ay as stille as stoon,
And evere gaped upward into the eir.

kiked gazed
woot knows
woodnesse madness
lewed ordinary
his bileve kan knows his Creed
marle-pit lime-pit
underspore thrust under
haspe he haaf it of heaved it off its hinges

This carpenter wende he were in despeir,
And hente hym by the sholdres myghtily,
And shook hym harde, and cride spitously,
'What! Nicholay! what, how! what, looke adoun!
Awake, and thenk on Cristes passioun!
I crouche thee from elves and fro wightes.'
Therwith the nyght-spel seyde he anon-rightes
On foure halves of the hous aboute,
And on the thresshfold of the dore withoute:
'Jhesu Crist and seïnt Benedight,
Blesse this hous from every wikked wight,
For nyghtes verye, the white *pater-noster*!
Where wentestow, seïnt Petres soster?'
   And atte laste this hende Nicholas
Gan for to sike soore, and seyde, 'Allas!
Shal al the world be lost eftsoones now?'
   This carpenter answerde, 'What seystow?
What! thynk on God, as we doon, men that swynke.'
   This Nicholas answerde, 'Fecche me drynke,
And after wol I speke in pryvetee
Of certeyn thyng that toucheth me and thee.
I wol telle it noon oother man, certeyn.'
   This carpenter goth doun, and comth ageyn,
And broghte of myghty ale a large quart;
And whan that ech of hem had dronke his part,
This Nicholas his dore faste shette,
And doun the carpenter by hym he sette.
   He seyde 'John, myn hooste, lief and deere,
Thou shalt upon thy trouthe swere me heere
That to no wight thou shalt this conseil wreye;
For it is Cristes conseil that I seye,
And if thou telle it man, thou art forlore;

crouche cross
nyghtes verye evil spirits
soster sister
eftsoones straightaway

[43]

For this vengeaunce thou shalt han therfore,
That if thou wreye me, thou shalt be wood.'
'Nay, Crist forbede it, for his hooly blood!'
Quod tho this sely man, 'I nam no labbe;
Ne, though I seye, I nam nat lief to gabbe.
Sey what thou wolt, I shal it nevere telle
To child ne wyf, by hym that harwed helle!'
     'Now John,' quod Nicholas, 'I wol nat lye;
I have yfounde in myn astrologye,
As I have looked in the moone bright,
That now a Monday next, at quarter nyght,
Shal falle a reyn, and that so wilde and wood,
That half so greet was nevere Noes flood.
This world,' he seyde, 'in lasse than an hour
Shal al be dreynt, so hidous is the shour.
Thus shal mankynde drenche, and lese hir lyf.'
     This carpenter answerde, 'Allas, my wyf!
And shal she drenche? allas, myn Alisoun!'
For sorwe of this he fil almoost adoun,
And seyde, 'Is ther no remedie in this cas?'
     'Why, yis, for Gode,' quod hende Nicholas,
'If thou wolt werken after loore and reed.
Thou mayst nat werken after thyn owene heed;
For thus seith Salomon, that was ful trewe,
"Werk al by conseil, and thou shalt nat rewe."
And if thou werken wolt by good conseil,
I undertake, withouten mast and seyl,
Yet shal I saven hire and thee and me.
Hastow nat herd hou saved was Noe,
Whan that oure Lord hadde warned hym biforn
That al the world with water sholde be lorn?'
     'Yis,' quod this Carpenter, 'ful yoore ago.'

wreye betray
wood mad
labbe blabbermouth

[44]

'Hastou nat herd,' quod Nicholas, 'also
The sorwe of Noe with his felaweshipe,
Er that he myghte gete his wyf to shipe?
Hym hadde be levere, I dar wel undertake
At thilke tyme, than alle his wetheres blake
That she hadde had a ship hirself allone.
And therfore, woostou what is best to doone?
This asketh haste, and of an hastif thyng
Men may nat preche or maken tariyng.
    Anon go gete us faste into this in
A knedyng trogh, or ellis a kymelyn,
For ech of us, but looke that they be large,
In which we mowe swymme as in a barge,
And han therinne vitaille suffisant
But for a day, — fy on the remenant!
The water shal aslake and goon away
Aboute pryme upon the nexte day.
But Robyn may nat wite of this, thy knave,
Ne eek thy mayde Gille I may nat save;
Axe nat why, for though thou aske me,
I wol nat tellen Goddes pryvetee.
Suffiseth thee, but if thy wittes madde,
To han as greet a grace as Noe hadde.
Thy wyf shal I wel saven, out of doute.
Go now thy wey, and speed thee heer-aboute.
    But whan thou hast, for hire and thee and me,
Ygeten us thise knedyng tubbes thre,
Thanne shaltow hange hem in the roof ful hye,
That no man of oure purveiaunce spye.
And whan thou thus hast doon, as I have seyd,
And hast oure vitaille faire in hem yleyd,

hadde be levere he had rather
wetheres sheep
kymelyn brewing tub
pryme nine o'clock
purveiaunce provision

[45]

And eek an ax, to smyte the corde atwo,
Whan that the water comth, that we may go,
And breke an hole an heigh, upon the gable,
Unto the gardyn-ward, over the stable,
That we may frely passen forth oure way,
Whan that the grete shour is goon away,
Thanne shaltou swymme as myrie, I undertake,
As dooth the white doke after hire drake.
Thanne wol I clepe, "How, Alison! how, John!
Be myrie, for the flood wol passe anon."
And thou wolt seyn, "Hayl, maister Nicholay!
Good morwe, I se thee well, for it is day."
And thanne shul we be lordes al oure lyf
Of al the world, as Noe and his wyf.

But of o thyng I warne thee ful right:
Be wel avysed on that ilke nyght
That we ben entred into shippes bord,
That noon of us ne speke nat a word,
Ne clepe, ne crie, but been in his preyere;
For it is Goddes owene heeste deere.

Thy wyf and thou moote hange fer atwynne;
For that bitwixe yow shal be no synne,
Namoore in lookyng than ther shal in deede.
This ordinance is seyd. Go, God thee speede!
Tomorwe at nyght, whan men ben alle aslepe,
Into oure knedyng-tubbes wol we crepe,
And sitten there, abidyng Goddes grace.
Go now thy wey, I have no lenger space
To make of this no lenger sermonyng.
Men seyn thus, "sende the wise, and sey no thyng":
Thou art so wys, it needeth thee nat teche.
Go, save oure lyf, and that I the biseche.'
This sely carpenter goth forth his wey.

heeste command
atwynne apart

[46]

Ful ofte he seide 'allas' and 'weylawey',
And to his wyf he tolde his pryvetee,
And she was war, and knew it bet than he,
What al this queynte cast was for to seye.
But nathelees she ferde as she wolde deye,
And seyde, 'Allas! go forth thy wey anon,
Help us to scape, or we been dede echon!
I am thy trewe, verray wedded wyf;
Go, deere spouse, and help to save oure lyf.'
   Lo, which a greet thyng is affeccioun!
Men may dyen of ymaginacioun,
So depe may impressioun be take.
This sely carpenter bigynneth quake;
Hym thynketh verraily that he may see
Noes flood come walwynge as the see
To drenchen Alisoun, his hony deere.
He wepeth, weyleth, maketh sory cheere;
He siketh with ful many a sory swogh;
He gooth and geteth hym a knedyng trogh,
And after that a tubbe and a kymelyn,
And pryvely he sente hem to his in,
And heng hem in the roof in pryvetee.
His owene hand he made laddres thre,
To clymben by the ronges and the stalkes
Unto the tubbes hangynge in the balkes,
And hem vitailled, bothe trogh and tubbe,
With breed and chese, and good ale in a jubbe,
Suffisynge right ynogh as for a day.
But er that he hadde maad al this array,
He sente his knave, and eek his wenche also,
Upon his nede to London for to go.
And on the Monday, whan it drow to nyght,

queynte cast strange contrivance
swogh sigh
kymelyn brewing-tub
jubbe jug

He shette his dore withoute candel-lyght,
And dressed alle thyng as it sholde be.
And shortly, up they clomben alle thre;
They seten stille wel a furlong way.
   'Now, *Pater-noster*, clom!' seyde Nicolay,
And 'clom', quod John, and 'clom', seyde Alisoun.
This carpenter seyde his devocioun,
And stille he sit, and biddeth his preyere,
Awaitynge on the reyn, if he it heere.
   The dede sleep, for wery bisynesse,
Fil on this carpenter right, as I gesse,
Aboute corfew-tyme, or litel moore;
For travaille of his goost he groneth soore,
And eft he routeth, for his heed myslay.
Doun of the laddre stalketh Nicholay,
And Alisoun ful softe adoun she spedde;
Withouten wordes mo they goon to bedde,
Ther as the carpenter is wont to lye.
Ther was the revel and the melodye;
And thus lith Alison and Nicholas,
In bisynesse of myrthe and of solas,
Til that the belle of laudes gan to rynge,
And freres in the chauncel gonne synge.
   This parissh clerk, this amorous Absolon,
That is for love alwey so wo bigon,
Upon the Monday was at Oseneye
With compaignye, hym to disporte and pleye,
And axed upon cas a cloisterer
Ful prively after John the carpenter;
And he drough hym apart out of the chirche,
And seyde, 'I noot, I saugh hym heere nat wirche
Syn Saterday; I trowe that he be went

clom keep quiet
laudes 4.30 a.m.
upon cas by chance

[48]

For tymber, ther oure abbot hath hym sent;
For he is wont for tymber for to go,
And dwellen at the grange a day to two;
Or elles he is at his hous, certeyn.
Where that he be, I kan nat soothly seyn.'
   This Absolon ful joly was and light,
And thoghte, 'Now is tyme to wake al nyght;
For sikirly I saugh hym nat stirynge
Aboute his dore, syn day bigan to sprynge.
   So moot I thryve, I shal, at cokkes crowe,
Ful pryvely knokken at his wyndowe
That stant ful lowe upon his boures wal.
To Alison now wol I tellen al
My love-longynge, for yet I shal nat mysse
That at the leeste wey I shal hire kisse.
Som maner confort shal I have, parfay.
My mouth hath icched al this longe day;
That is a signe of kissyng atte leeste.
Al nyght me mette eek I was at a feeste.
Therfore I wol go slepe an houre or tweye,
And al the nyght thanne wol I wake and pleye.'
   Whan that the firste cok hath crowe, anon
Up rist this joly lovere Absolon,
And hym arraieth gay, at poynt-devys.
But first he cheweth greyn and lycorys,
To smellen sweete, er he hadde kembd his heer.
Under his tonge a trewe-love he beer,
For therby wende he to ben gracious.
He rometh to the carpenteres hous,
And stille he stant under the shot-wyndowe –
Unto his brest it raughte, it was so lowe –
And softe he cougheth with a semy soun:

me mette I dreamed
greyn cardamoms
semy small

'What do ye, hony-comb, sweete Alisoun,
My faire bryd, my sweete cynamome?
Awaketh, lemman myn, and speketh to me!
Wel litel thynken ye upon my wo,
That for youre love I swete ther I go.
No wonder is thogh that I swelte and swete;
I moorne as dooth a lamb after the tete.
Ywis, lemman, I have swich love-longynge,
That lik a turtel trewe is my moornynge.
I may nat ete na moore than a mayde.'
   'Go fro the wyndow, Jakke fool,' she sayde;
'As help me God, it wol nat be "com ba me".
I love another – and elles I were to blame –
Wel bet than thee, by Jhesu, Absolon.
Go forth thy wey, or I wol caste a ston,
And lat me slepe, a twenty devel wey!'
   'Allas,' quod Absolon, 'and weylawey,
That trewe love was evere so yvel biset!
Thanne kysse me, syn it may be no bet,
For Jhesus love, and for the love of me.'
   'Wiltow thanne go thy wey therwith?' quod she.
   'Ye, certes, lemman,' quod this Absolon.
   'Thanne make thee redy,' quod she, 'I come anon.'
And unto Nicholas she seyde stille,
'Now hust, and thou shalt laughen al thy fille.'
   This Absolon doun sette hym on his knees
And seyde, 'I am a lord at alle degrees;
For after this I hope ther cometh moore.
Lemman, thy grace, and sweete bryd, thyn oore!'
   The wyndow she undoth, and that in haste.
'Have do,' quod she, 'com of, and speed thee faste,
Lest that oure neighebores thee espie.'

swelte swelter
come ba me come kiss me
hust hush

This Absolon gan wype his mouth ful drie.
Derk was the nyght as pich, or as the cole,
And at the wyndow out she putte hir hole,
And Absolon, hym fil no bet ne wers,
But with his mouth he kiste hir naked ers
Ful savourly, er he were war of this.
Abak he stirte, and thoughte it was amys,
For wel he wiste a womman hath no berd.
He felte a thyng al rough and long yherd,
And seyde, 'Fy! allas! what have I do?'
    'Tehee!' quod she, and clapte the wyndow to.
And Absolon gooth forth a sory pas.
    'A berd! a berd!' quod hende Nicholas,
'By Goddes corpus, this goth faire and weel.'
    This sely Absolon herde every deel,
And on his lippe he gan for anger byte,
And to hymself he seyde, 'I shal thee quyte.'
    Who rubbeth now, who froteth now his lippes
With dust, with sond, with straw, with clooth, with chippes,
But Absolon, that seith ful ofte, 'Allas!'
'My soule bitake I unto Sathanas,
But me were levere than al this toun,' quod he,
'Of this despit awroken for to be.
Allas,' quod he, 'allas, I ne hadde ybleynt!'
His hoote love was coold and al yqueynt;
For fro that tyme that he hadde kist hir ers,
Of paramours he sette nat a kers;
For he was heeled of his maladie.
Ful ofte paramours he gan deffie,
And weep as dooth a child that is ybete.
A softe paas he wente over the strete

fil no bet ne wers it befell him
quyte repay
froteth rubs
levere than al I had rather
I ne hadde ybleynt! I wish I hadn't!
A softe paas quietly

Until a smyth men cleped daun Gerveys,
That in his forge smythed plough harneys;
He sharpeth shaar and kultour bisily.
This Absolon knokketh al esily,
And seyde, 'Undo, Gerveys, and that anon.'
 'What, who artow?' 'It am I, Absolon.'
'What, Absolon! for Cristes sweete tree,
Why rise ye so rathe? ey, *benedicitee*!
What eyleth yow? Som gay gerl, God it woot,
Hath broght yow thus upon the viritoot.
By seinte Note, ye woot wel what I mene.'
    This Absolon ne roghte nat a bene
Of al his pley; no word agayn he yaf;
He hadde moore tow on his distaf
Than Gerveys knew, and seyde, 'Freend so deere,
That hoote kultour in the chymenee heere,
As lene it me, I have therwith to doone,
And I wol brynge it thee agayn ful soone.'
    Gerveys answerde, 'Certes, were it gold,
Or in a poke nobles alle untold,
Thou sholdest have, as I am trewe smyth.
Ey, Cristes foo! what wol ye do therwith?'
    'Therof,' quod Absolon, 'be as he may.
I shal wel telle it thee to-morwe day' —
And caughte the kultour by the colde stele.
Ful softe out at the dore he gan to stele,
And wente unto the carpenteris wal.
He cogheth first, and knokketh therwithal
Upon the wyndowe, right as he dide er.

kultour ploughshares
viritoot so quickly
ne roghte nat a bene didn't give a damn
tow on his distaf business in hand
in a poke nobles gold coins in a sack
Cristes foo the devil

This Alison answerde, 'Who is ther
That knokketh so? I warante it a theef.'
  'Why, nay,' quod he, 'God woot, my sweete leef,
I am thyn Absolon, my deerelyng.
Of gold,' quod he, 'I have thee broght a ryng.
My mooder yaf it me, so God me save;
Ful fyn it is, and therto wel ygrave.
This wol I yeve thee, if thou me kisse.'
  This Nicholas was risen for to pisse,
And thoughte he wolde amenden al the jape;
He sholde kisse his ers er that he scape.
And up the wyndowe dide he hastily,
And out his ers he putteth pryvely
Over the buttok, to the haunche-bon;
And therwith spak this clerk, this Absolon,
'Spek, sweete bryd, I noot nat where thou art.'
  This Nicholas anon leet fle a fart,
As greet as it had been a thonder-dent,
That with the strook he was almoost yblent;
And he was redy with his iren hoot,
And Nicholas amydde the ers he smoot.
  Of gooth the skyn an hande-brede aboute,
The hoote kultour brende so his toute,
And for the smert he wende for to dye.
As he were wood, for wo he gan to crye,
'Help! water! water! help, for Goddes herte!'
  This carpenter out of his slomber sterte,
And herde oon crien 'water' as he were wood,
And thoughte, 'Allas, now comth Nowelis flood!'
He sit hym up withouten wordes mo,
And with his ax he smoot the corde atwo,

ygrave engraved
yblent blinded
Of gooth the skyn off goes the skin
toute backside
wood mad

And doun gooth al; he foond neither to selle
Ne breed ne ale, til he cam to the celle
Upon the floor, and ther aswowne he lay.
   Up stirte hire Alison and Nicholay,
And criden 'out' and 'harrow' in the strete.
The neighebores, bothe smale and grete,
In ronnen for to gauren on this man,
That yet aswowne lay, bothe pale and wan,
For with the fal he brosten hadde his arm.
But stonde he moste unto his owene harm;
For whan he spak, he was anon bore doun
With hende Nicholas and Alisoun.
They tolden every man that he was wood,
He was agast so of Nowelis flood
Thurgh fantasie, that of his vanytee
He hadde yboght hym knedyng tubbes thre,
And hadde hem hanged in the roof above;
And that he preyed hem, for Goddes love,
To sitten in the roof, *par compaignye.*
   The folk gan laughen at his fantasye;
Into the roof they kiken and they gape,
And turned al his harm unto a jape.
For what so that this carpenter answerde,
It was for noght, no man his reson herde.
With othes grete he was so sworn adoun
That he was holde wood in al the toun;
For every clerk anonright heeld with other.
They seyde, 'The man is wood, my leeve brother';
And every wight gan laughen at this stryf.
Thus swyved was this carpenteris wyf,
For al his kepyng and his jalousye;

Ne breed ne ale he didn't stop
celle floorboard
gauren stare
gape gaze
wood mad

And Absolon hath kist hir nether yë;
And Nicholas is scalded in the towte.
This tale is doon, and God save al the rowte!

GEOFFREY CHAUCER

Hogyn

Hogyn came to bower's door,
Hogyn came to bower's door,
He tirled upon the pin for love,
    Hum, ha, trill go bell,
He tirled upon the pin for love,
    Hum, ha, trill go bell.

Up she rose and let him in,
Up she rose and let him in,
She had awent she had worshipped all her kin,
    Hum, ha, trill go bell,
She had awent she had worshipped all her kin,
    Hum, ha, trill go bell.

When they were to bed brought,
When they were to bed brought,
The old churl he could do nought,
    Hum, ha, trill go bell,
The old churl he could do nought.
    Hum, ha, trill go bell.

Go ye forth to yonder window,
Go ye forth to yonder window,
And I will come to you within a throw,
    Hum, ha, trill go bell,
And I will come to you within a throw,
    Hum, ha, trill go bell.

When she him at the window wist,
When she him at the window wist,
She turned out her arse and that he kissed,
    Hum, ha, trill go bell,
She turned out her arse and that he kissed,
    Hum, ha, trill go bell.

Iwis, leman, ye do me wrong,
Iwis, leman, ye do me wrong,
Or else your breath is wonder strong,
   Hum, ha, trill go bell,
Or else your breath is wonder strong,
   Hum, ha, trill go bell.

ANON.

Comin' Throu the Rye

O gin a body meet a body,
  Comin' throu the rye,
Gin a body fuck a body,
  Need a body cry?
    Comin' throu the rye, my jo,
      An' comin' throu the rye;
    She fand a staun o staunin graith
      Comin' throu the rye.

Gin a body meet a body
  Comin' throu the glen,
Gin a body fuck a body,
  Need the warld ken?
    Comin' throu the rye, etc.

Gin a body meet a body
  Comin' throu the grain,
Gin a body fuck a body,
  Cunt's a body's ain.
    Comin' throu the rye, etc.

Gin a body meet a body
  By a body's sel,
Whatna body fucks a body,
  Wad a body tell?
    Comin' throu the rye, etc.

Mony a body meets a body
  They darena weel avow;
Mony a body fucks a body,
  Ye wadna think it true.
    Comin, throu the rye, my jo,
      An' comin throu the rye,
    She fand a staun o staunin graith
      Comin' throu the rye.

ROBERT BURNS

The Songs of the PWD Man

We were not born to survive, alas,
But to step on the gas.

ANDREI VOZNESENSKY

I

I'll bet you're bloody jealous, you codgers in UK,
Waiting for your hearses while I'm having it away
With girls like black Bathshebas who sell their milky curds
At kerbside markets out of done-up-fancy gourds,
Black as tar-macadam, skin shining when it's wet
From washing or from kissing like polished Whitby jet.
They're lovely, these young lasses. Those colonial DO's
Knew what they were up to when they upped and chose
These slender, tall Fulanis like Rowntrees coffee creams
To keep in wifeless villas. No Boy Scout's fleapit dreams
Of bedding Brigitte Bardot could ever better these.
One shy kiss from this lot has me shaking at the knees.
It's not that they're casual, they're just glad of the lifts
I give them between markets and in gratitude give gifts
Like sips of fresh cow-juice off a calabash spoon.
But I'm subject to diarrhoea, so I'd just as soon
Have a feel of those titties that hang down just below
That sort of beaded bolero of deep indigo blue;
And to the woven wrapper worn exactly navel high,
All's bare but for ju-jus and, where it parts, a thigh
Sidles through the opening with a bloom like purple grapes.
So it's not all that surprising that some lecherous apes
Take rather rough advantage, mostly blacks and Lebanese,
Though I've heard it tell as well that it were one of these
That *white* Police Inspector fancied and forced down
At the back of barracks in the sleazy part of town.
Well, of course, she hollered and her wiry brothers ran
And set rabid packs of bushdogs on the desperate man.

[60]

He perished black all over and foaming at the mouth.
They're nomadic, these Fulanis, driving to the South
That special hump-backed cow they have, and when they're
  on trek,
They leave wigwamloads of women, and by blooming heck,
I drive in their direction, my right foot pressed right down
Laying roads and ladies up as far as Kano town.
Though I'm not your socialistic, go-native-ite type chap
With his flapping, nig-nog dresses and his dose of clap,
I have my finer feelings and I'd like to make it clear
I'm not just itchy fingers and a senile lecher's leer.
I have my qualms of conscience and shower *silver*, if you
  please,
To their lepers and blind beggars kipping under trees.
They're agile enough, those cripples, scrabbling for the
  coins,
But not half so bloody agile as those furry little groins
I grope for through strange garments smelling of dye-pits
As I gaze my grizzly whiskers on those black, blancmangy
  tits.
I don't do bad for sixty. You can stuff your Welfare State.
You can't get girls on National Health and I won't
  masturbate.
They're pleased with my performance. I'm satisfied with
  theirs.
No! I think they're very beautiful, although their hair's
A bit off-putting, being rough like panscrub wires,
But bums like melons, matey, lips like lorry tyres.
They all know old Roller Coaster. And, oh dear, ugh!
To think I ever nuzzled on a poor white woman's dug,
Pale, collapsed and shrivelled like a week-old mushroom
  swept
Up at Kirkgate City Markets. Jesus bleeding wept!
Back to sporting, smoky Yorkshire! I dread retirement age
And the talking drum send-off at the Lagos landing stage.

Out here I'm as sprightly as old George Formby's uke.
I think of Old Folk's England and, honest, I could puke.
Here I'm getting younger and I don't need monkey glands,
Just a bit of money and a pair of young, black hands.
I used to cackle at that spraycart trying to put down
That grass and them tansies that grew all over town.
Death's like the Corporation for old men back in Leeds,
Shooting out its poisons and choking off the weeds.
But I'm like them tansies or a stick cut in the bush
And shoved in for a beanpole that suddenly grows lush
With new leafage before the garden lad's got round
To plucking the beans off and digging up the ground.
Yes, better to put the foot down, go fast, accelerate,
Than shrivel on your arses, mope and squawk and wait
For Death to drop the darkness over twittering age
Like a bit of old blanket on a parrot's cage.

II

Life's movement and life's danger and not a sit-down post.
There's skeleton cars and lorries from Kano to the coast;
Skeletons but not wasted, those flashy Chevie fins
Honed up for knife blades or curled for muezzins
To megaphone the *Koran* from their mud mosques and call
The sun down from its shining with their caterwaul.
But it's not just native say-so; it's stark, realistic fact;
The road's a royal python's dark digestive tract.
And I expect that it'll get me one rainy season night,
That sudden, skating backwheel skid across the laterite,
Or a lorry without headlights, GOD IS LOVE up on the cab,
Might impale me on my pistons like a raw *kebab*.
Smash turned into landscape, ambulance, that's that,
A white corpse starkers like a suddenly skinned cat.

As kids when we came croppers, there were always some
old dears

Who'd come and pick us up and wipe off blood and tears,
And who'd always use the same daft words, as they tried to
  console,
Pointing to cobble, path or flagstone: *Look at the hole
You've made falling.* I want a voice with that soft tone,
Disembodied Yorkshire like my mother's on the phone,
As the cook puts down some flowers and the smallboy
  scrapes the spade,
To speak as my epitaph: *Look at the hole he's made.*

TONY HARRISON

Cod-Liver Oil and the Orange Juice

Out of the East there came a hard man,
O-ho, all the way frae Brigton,
O-ho, Glory Hallelujah,
Cod-liver oil and the orange juice.

He went into a pub and came out paralytic,
O-ho, VP and cider,
O-ho, a hell of a mixture,
Cod-liver oil and the orange juice.

In the dancing he met Hairy Mary,
O-ho, the floor o' the Gorbals,
O-ho, Glory Hallelujah,
Cod-liver oil and the orange juice.

He said to her, 'Mary, hen, are you dancing?'
'Oh no, it's just the way I'm standing.'
O-ho, Glory Hallelujah,
Cod-liver oil and the orange juice.

He said to her, 'Mary, you're one in a million.'
'O-ho, and so's your chances.'
O-ho, Glory Hallelujah,
Cod-liver oil and the orange juice.

He said to her, 'Mary, can I run you home?'
'Oh no, I've got a pair of sand-shoes.'
O-ho, hell of a funny,
Cod-liver oil and the orange juice.

Down through the back close and into the dunny,
O-ho, it wasna for the first time.
O-ho, it wouldna be the last time,
Cod-liver oil and the orange juice.

Oot came her mammy, she was going to the kludgie,
O-ho, he buggered off sharpish,
O-ho, Glory Hallelujah,
Cod-liver oil and the orange juice.

Hairy Mary's looking for her hard man,
O-ho, he's joined the Foreign Legion.
A-ha, Sahara under a camel,
Cod-liver oil and the orange juice.

Hairy Mary had a little baby,
O-ho, its faither's in the army,
O-ho, Glory Hallelujah,
Cod-liver oil and the orange juice.

HAMISH IMLACH
(MacDougall/Imlach, *Heathside Music*)

The Thing That People Do

When God created Paradise,
As every child can tell,
He placed old Adam gardener
With a woman there as well.
Said God: 'Enjoy yourself, me lad,
And enjoy your woman, too,
But never let me catch you at
The thing that people do.'

Oh the thing that people do,
The thing that people do:
It's long-winded and it's difficult,
Like changing trains at Crewe,
So go enjoy yourself, me lad,
And enjoy your woman, too,
But never let me catch you at
The thing that people do!

'Lay off young Alcibiades,'
The Athenian court did say,
'And Socrates, just tell us why
Our lads turn out that way?
Euripides? Eumenides!
It's an old, old tale but true.
We'll dose you up with hemlock for
The thing that people do.'

Oh the thing some people do,
The thing some people do,
The thing you need the ointment for
If you don't want a botcheroo.
Euripides? Eumenides!
It's an old, old tale but true
And we'll dose you up with hemlock for
The thing some people do.

Leander, growing weary, cried:
'This is quite beyond a joke.
It's saltier than the Hellespont.
I'll try just one more stroke,
But I'm in it up to the shoulder-blades
(I should have brought a canoe).
It'll come to a sticky end all right,
This thing that people do.'

Oh the thing that people do,
The thing that people do!
It's deep and wet and dangerous,
With more than a whiff of glue.
But you're in it up to your shoulder-blades
And you wish you'd brought a canoe.
It'll come to a sticky end all right,
The thing that people do.

Once Mrs Patrick Campbell
Was alone with Bernard Shaw
She apologized profusely
As she dragged him to the floor:
'I'm Shavian under the armpits,
I'm Shavian through and through,
But what's the point without a bit of
The thing that Shavians do?'

Oh the thing that Shavians do,
The thing that Shavians do,
The thing they do with vegetables,
It tastes like Irish stew.
I'm Shavian under the armpits,
I'm Shavian through and through,
But what's the point without a bit of
The thing that Shavians do?

What Oscar Wilde and Bosie did
With their respective tools
Was certainly below the belt
And against the Queensberry rules.
'Oh Oscar Fingal O'Flaherty, dear,
Is it up to me, or to you?
Either way it's a bit *outré*,
The thing that aesthetes do.'

Oh the thing that aesthetes do,
The thing that aesthetes do.
Some do it with great style. They use
A pubic hair shampoo.
But others simply steep the sheets
Now and then in Reckitt's Blue.
Whatever way, it's a bit *outré*,
The thing that aesthetes do.

And then there was Havelock Ellis
Who loved his consommé,
But whenever he tried to drink it
His beard got in the way.
Beards are more trouble than they're worth
When you're playing peekaboo
And hair gets simply everywhere in
The thing that people do.

Oh the thing that people do,
The thing that people do:
Such beastly consequences from
That fatal interview
When neither knows what the other wants
In the game of peekaboo
And everything gets everywhere in
The thing that people do.

When Lou Andreas-Salomé
Made her bid for Sigmund Freud,
She found his Pleasure Principle
Grotesquely unemployed.
Said Freud: 'You did for Nietzsche
And you did for Rilke, Lou,
But mate, I've learned to sublimate
The thing that people do.'

Oh the thing that people do,
The thing that people do.
Vienna is obsessed with it,
Like monkeys at the zoo.
It was good enough for Nietzsche.
It was great for Rilke, Lou,
But mate, I've learned to sublimate
The thing that people do.

When Lawrence of Arabia
Was roughed up by a Turk
He made this bold confession
As the brute got down to work:
'I can do it with an earmuff,
I'm not bad with a shoe,
But tell me, how do people fit
In this thing that people do?'

Oh the thing that people do,
The thing that people do!
It's easy when you're on your tod,
Much trickier when there's two.
There's comfort in an earmuff.
There's triumph in a shoe.
But I just can't see how people fit
In this thing that people do.

Leda was always swanning about
And Irene gave in to Soames.
Ginger did it with William
And Watson did it with Holmes.
The Queen of England has done it
And someone does it with you:
But why on earth do they do it,
The thing that people do?

Oh the thing that people do,
The thing that people do.
Why did you have to remind us?
Why isn't the thing taboo?
Everyone does it to someone
And someone does it to you,
But why, why, WHY do they do it,
The thing that people do?

JOHN FULLER AND JAMES FENTON

A Ramble in St James's Park

Much wine had passed, with grave discourse
Of who fucks who, and who does worse
(Such as you usually do hear
From those that diet at the Bear),
When I, who still take care to see
Drunkenness relieved by lechery,
Went out into St James's Park
To cool my head and fire my heart.
But though St James has th'honour on 't,
'Tis consecrate to prick and cunt.
There, by a most incestuous birth,
Strange woods spring from the teeming earth;
For they relate how heretofore,
When ancient Pict began to whore,
Deluded of his assignation
(Jilting, it seems, was then in fashion),
Poor pensive lover, in this place
Would frig upon his mother's face;
Whence rows of mandrakes tall did rise
Whose lewd tops fucked the very skies.
Each imitative branch does twine
In some loved fold of Aretine,
And nightly now beneath their shade
Are buggeries, rapes, and incests made.
Unto this all-sin-sheltering grove
Whores of the bulk and the alcove,
Great ladies, chambermaids and drudges,
The ragpicker, and heiress trudges.
Carmen, divines, great lords, and tailors,
Prentices, poets, pimps, and jailers,
Footmen, fine fops do here arrive,
And here promiscuously they swive.

bulk shop front

Along these hallowed walks it was
That I beheld Corinna pass.
Whoever had been by to see
The proud disdain she cast on me
Through charming eyes, he would have swore
She dropped from heaven that very hour,
Forsaking the divine abode
In scorn of some despairing god.
But mark what creatures women are:
How infinitely vile, when fair!
   Three knights o' th' elbow and the slur
With wriggling tails made up to her.
   The first was of your Whitehall blades,
Near kin t' th' Mother of the Maids;
Graced by whose favour he was able
To bring a friend t' th' Waiters' table,
Where he had heard Sir Edward Sutton
Say how the King loved Banstead mutton;
Since when he'd ne'er be brought to eat
By 's good will any other meat.
   In this, as well as all the rest,
He ventures to do like the best,
But wanting common sense, th'ingredient
In choosing well not least expedient,
Converts abortive imitation
To universal affectation.
Thus he not only eats and talks
But feels and smells, sits down and walks
Nay looks, and lives, and loves by rote,
In an old tawdry birthday coat.
   The second was a Gray's Inn wit,
A great inhabiter of the pit,
Where critic-like he sits and squints,
Steals pocket handkerchiefs, and hints,

th' elbow and the slur cheating at dice

From 's neighbour, and the comedy,
To court, and pay, his landlady.
    The third, a lady's eldest son
Within few years of twenty-one,
Who hopes from his propitious fate,
Against he comes to his estate,
By these two worthies to be made
A most accomplished tearing blade.
    One, in a strain 'twixt tune and nonsense,
Cries, 'Madam, I have loved you long since.
Permit me your fair hand to kiss';
When at her mouth her cunt cries, 'Yes!'
In short, without much more ado,
Joyful and pleased, away she flew,
And with these three confounded asses
From park to hackney coach she passes.
    So a proud bitch does lead about
Of humble curs and amorous rout,
Who most obsequiously do hunt
The savoury scent of salt-swoln cunt.
Some power more patient now relate
The sense of this surprising fate.
Gods! that a thing admired by me
Should fall to so much infamy.
Had she picked out, to rub her arse on,
Some stiff-pricked clown or well-hung parson,
Each job of whose spermatic sluice
Had filled her cunt with wholesome juice,
I the proceeding should have praised
In hope sh' had quenched a fire I raised.
Such natural freedoms are but just:
There's something generous in mere lust.
But to turn damned abandoned jade
When neither head nor tail persuade;
To be a whore in understanding,
A passive pot for fools to spend in!

[73]

The devil played booty, sure, with thee
To bring a blot on infamy.
   But why am I, of all mankind,
To so severe a fate designed?
Ungrateful! Why this treachery
To humble, fond, believing me,
Who gave you privilege above
The nice allowances of love?
Did I ever refuse to bear
The meanest part your lust could spare?
When your lewd cunt came spewing home
Drenched with the seed of half the town,
My dram of sperm was supped up after
For the digestive surfeit water.
Full gorgèd at another time
With a vast meal of nasty slime
Which your devouring cunt had drawn
From porters' backs and footmen's brawn,
I was content to serve you up
My ballock-full for your grace cup,
Nor ever thought it an abuse
While you had pleasure for excuse –
You that could make my heart away
For noise and colour, and betray
The secrets of my tender hours
To such knight-errant paramours,
When, leaning on your faithless breast,
Wrapped in security and rest,
Soft kindness all my powers did move,
And reason lay dissolved in love!
   May stinking vapours choke your womb
Such as the men you dote upon!
May your depravèd appetite,
That could in whiffling fools delight,
Beget such frenzies in your mind
You may go mad for the north wind,

And fixing all your hopes upon 't
To have him bluster in your cunt,
Turn up your longing arse t' th' air
And perish in a wild despair!
But cowards shall forget to rant,
Schoolboys to frig, old whores to paint;
The Jesuits' fraternity
Shall leave the use of buggery;
Crab-louse, inspired with grace divine,
From earthly cod to heaven shall climb;
Physicians shall believe in Jesus,
And disobedience cease to please us,
Ere I desist with all my power
To plague this woman and undo her.
But my revenge will best be timed
When she is married that is limed.
In that most lamentable state
I'll make her feel my scorn and hate:
Pelt her with scandals, truth or lies,
And her poor cur with jealousies,
Till I have torn him from her breech,
While she whines like a dog-drawn bitch;
Loathed and despised, kick'd out o' th' Town
Into some dirty hole alone,
To chew the cud of misery
And know she owes it all to me.
   And may no woman better thrive
That dares profane the cunt I swive!

JOHN WILMOT, EARL OF ROCHESTER

You Jane

At night fart a guinness smell against the wife
who snuggles up to me after I've given her one
after the Dog and Fox. It's all muscle. You can punch
my gut and wait for ever till I flinch. Try it.
Man of the house. Master in my own home. Solid.

Look at that bicep. Dinner on the table
and a clean shirt, but I respect her point of view.
She's borne me two in eight years, knows
when to button it. Although she's run a bit to fat
she still bends over of a weekend in suspenders.

This is the life. Australia next year and bugger
the mother-in-law. Just feel those thighs.
Karate keeps me like granite. Strength of an ox.
I can cope with the ale no problem. Pints
with the lads, a laugh, then home to her.

She says Did you dream, love? I never
dream. Sleep is as black as a good jar.
I wake half-conscious with a hard-on, shove it in.
She don't complain. When I feel, I feel here
where the purple vein in my neck throbs.

CAROL ANN DUFFY

Life Presents a Dismal Picture

Air: 'Deutschland über Alles'

Life presents a dismal picture,
All around is toil and gloom;
Father has an anal stricture,
Mother has a fallen womb.
In the corner squats Jemima,
Never laughs and rarely smiles.
What a wretched occupation,
Cracking ice for father's piles!

Uncle Henry was transported
For a homosexual crime,
And the housemaid has aborted
For the twenty-second time.
Our new baby's no exception
For he's always having fits.
Every time he cries he pukes and
Every time he laughs he shits.

Cousin Joseph won the Hackney
Masturbation marathon.
But he died of self-expression
When he buggered Uncle John.
Bert the postman called this morning,
Stuck his penis through the door.
We could not, despite endearment,
Get it out till half-past four.

In a small brown-paper parcel
Wrapped in a mysterious way
Is an imitation arsehole
Grandad uses twice a day.
From the shithouse hear him yelling
(No one helps the ancient clown);
Hours ago he pushed the plug up
And he cannot get it down.

ANON.

YOUTH AND AGE

Babies in Their Mothers' Arms

Babies in their mothers' arms
Exercise their budding charms
On their fingers and their toes,
Striving ever to enclose
In the circle of their will
Objects disobedient still,
But the boy comes fast enough
To the limits of self-love,
And the adult learns what small
Forces rally at his call.
Large and paramount the State
That will not co-operate
With the Duchy of his mind:
All his lifetime he will find
Swollen knee or aching tooth
Hostile to his quest for truth;
Never will his prick belong
To his world of right and wrong,
Nor its values comprehend
Who is foe and who is friend.

W. H. AUDEN

The Ram

He jangles his keys in the rain
and I follow like a lamb.
His house is as smoky as a dive.
We go straight downstairs to his room.

I lie on his bed and watch him
undress. His orange baseball jacket,
all the way from Ontario,
drops to the floor — THE RAMS, in felt,

arched across the hunky back.
He unzips his calf-length
Star-walkers, his damp black Levi's,
and adjusts his loaded modelling-pouch:

he stands before me in his socks —
as white as bridesmaids,
little daisies, driven snow.
John Wayne watches from the wall

beside a shelf-ful of pistols.
Well, he says, *d'you like it?*
All I can think of is Granny,
how she used to shake her head,

when I stood by her bed on Sundays,
so proud in my soap-smelling
special frock, and say *Ah,*
Bless your little cotton socks!

SELIMA HILL

On the Happy Corydon and Phyllis

Young Corydon and Phyllis
   Sat in a lovely grove,
Contriving crowns of lilies,
   Repeating toys of love,
And something else, but what I dare not name.

But as they were a-playing,
   She ogled so the swain;
It saved her plainly saying
   Let's kiss to ease our pain:
And something else, but what I dare not name.

A thousand times he kissed her,
   Laying her on the green;
But as he farther pressed her,
   A pretty leg was seen:
And something else, but what I dare not name.

So many beauties viewing,
   His ardour still increased;
And greater joys pursuing,
   He wandered o'er her breast:
And something else, but what I dare not name.

A last effort she trying,
   His passion to withstand;
Cried, but it was faintly crying,
   Pray take away your hand:
And something else, but what I dare not name.

Young Corydon grown bolder,
   The minutes would improve;
This is the time, he told her,
   To show you how I love;
And something else, but what I dare not name.

The nymph seemed almost dying,
  Dissolved in amorous heat;
She kissed and told him sighing,
  My dear your love is great:
And something else, but what I dare not name.

But Phyllis did recover
  Much sooner than the swain;
She blushing asked her lover,
  Shall we not kiss again:
And something else, but what I dare not name.

Thus Love his revels keeping,
  'Til Nature at a stand;
From talk they fell to sleeping,
  Holding each others hand;
And something else, but what I dare not name.

SIR CHARLES SEDLEY

Double Date

Myself and Curtis Dean are seniors together, –
   half- and full-backs, junior-varsity teams.
Dean and I have fun, all sortsa weather
   sharing similar sexual dreams.

Curt and I do quite a lota double-dating,
   specially on Saturday night, –
lotsa heavy-loving, (some x-rating),
   fanTAStic freeform farout delights.

Last Senior Prom he picks me up 7.30.
   We get Jane, – and friend (some unknown dame):
four of us, – crocked. Start talking-dirty,
   kick-off in the double-dating game.

First: breast-fondling. Then light n'lively kissing;
   next: pet-to-climax, (tongue & ear).
Then, partial-stripping. Still, something's missing.
   Jane plays the field; her friend's full o' fear.

Curt, – (he only ASKed her), – just suggesting shyly:
   'Stroke my pecker, please.' (Inside his pants.)
She gets sore: 'I'm a NICE girl!' (A lie.) She
   weeps; we'll miss that old high-school dance.

I laugh like hell, but Curt's bitched and bitter;
   starts up his car; gravel flies, wheels squeal.
Janes takes HER side. I sure coulda hit her.
   Curtis drives fast feeling one real heel.

We walk 'em to their door. They slamit, not speaking.
   Dean says: 'You drive. I'm too pissed to move.'
Must we go home yet? We stall there, seeking
   some real outlet for unrequited love.

Parked on a side-street for more serious-drinking
   Curt grins: 'I'm horny.' 'Beat-off,' I said. —
much the same we both of us were thinking;
   easier when formal-dress is shed.

Dumb simple hand-jobs aren't so all-fired thrilling.
   Dean sighs: 'I'll do you if you do me.'
Chances being caught queer can be chilling;
   we were jet-propelled on liberty.

Agreed on next steps albeit kinda risky;
   stripped bare-ass on that slippery back-seat.
Man o Man! That full-back's prime-time frisky!
   Mutual release is mor'n beating-meat.

But just like it was when those chicks got us started, —
   no chance of rocks-off. Fate interferes.
Headlights spot our tangle. We get us parted.
   Nudity unknots two bare-assed queers.

Flashlight glares hot on our raw frank condition;
   'What's goin' ON here?' inquires this Cop.
'Officer, we're drunk, sir.' Rank submission.
   Cop snaps: 'Curtis Dean! This gotta STOP!'

Yup. We're illegal. Policeman put it clearly:
   (he knows Dean's dad; acts paternally):
'Just pull your pants on,' proposing merely:
   'You're too drunk to drive, boys. Follow me.'

To Curt's house, bingo! Police-escort protection!
   Real motherly is Curt Dean's mother:
'You poor lambs look TIRED!' With no objection
   we bounce to bed. No further bother.

LINCOLN KIRSTEIN

Tryst

Me and Gib likes it here – always comes of a night,
no one else gets here, see. That's his Great-Grandad's stone.
Gassed, *he* was; got sent home from one of them *old* wars.
    Tommy, they called him.

We sprayed HARTLEPOOL WANKERS on one of them. Great!
This is the newest one – sad it is, really, it's
some little ten-year-old girlie's. Them plastic daffs
    look very nice, though.

He likes to get me down in the long weeds between
two of them marble things – I can see ivy sprout
on the cross by his head. He makes me squiggle when
    he sticks his hand up.

He works at one of them mills what makes cattle food.
He stacks the sacks. You should see them tattoos on his
arms when he flexes them. There is a big red heart
    with TRUE LOVE on it.

He runs the Packer-thing all on his own, he does.
We've saving up to get married and have a big
do like that big snob that works in our office had
    (Crystal, her name is).

I let him do what he wants – he pretends that he's
the Ripper, sometimes, and get me down on a grave;
then what he does with his hands feels like scurrying
    rats up my T-shirt.

When we're saved up enough, we're going to wed in church.
This is alright, though – at least in the summertime.
They don't pay poor Gib much, stacking them heavy sacks
    off the conveyor.

PETER READING

Low Scene

The apprentice – fifteen, ugly, not too thin,
Nice in a softish uncouth way, dull skin,
Bright deep-set eyes – blue overalls – pulls out
His springy, stiff, well-tuned, quite man-sized spout
And rams the boss's wife – big but still good,
Flopped on the bed's edge – what an attitude! –
Legs up, breasts out, one hand parting her placket.
To see him crush her arse under his jacket
And quickstep forward more than back, it's clear
He's not afraid how deep he plants his gear
Or if the lady fruits – she doesn't care –
Isn't her trusty cuckold always there? –
So when she reaches, as he shoots his goal,
That rapture of the body as a whole,
She cries, 'You've made a child, I feel it, love,
And love you more,' and after his last shove
Adds, 'Look, the christening sweets,' and squats and tries
To heft and kiss his bollocks through his flies.

PAUL VERLAINE
translated by Alistair Elliot

A Song of a Young Lady to Her Ancient Lover

Ancient person, for whom I
All the flattering youth defy,
Long it be ere thou grow old,
Aching, shaking, crazy cold,
But still continue as thou art,
Ancient person of my heart.

On thy withered lips and dry,
Which like barren furrows lie,
Brooding kisses I will pour
Shall thy youthful heat restore.
Such kind showers in Autumn fall,
And a second Spring recall,
Nor from thee will ever part,
Ancient person of my heart.

Thy nobler part, which but to name,
In our sex would be counted shame,
By Age's frozen grasp possessed,
From his ice shall be released,
And, soothed by my reviving hand,
In former warmth and vigour stand.
All a Lover's wish can reach,
For thy joy my Love shall teach,
And for thy pleasure shall improve
All that Art can add to Love.
Yet still I love thee without art,
Ancient person of my heart.

JOHN WILMOT, EARL OF ROCHESTER

To Madame * * *

When you wrap thighs around my head
And hug, or squeeze them round my bum,
Cramming my craw with a great spread
Of your astringent youthful come,

Or taking with your glistening slot
(Just made for master keys) a nip
Out of my bud (that's all I've got,
But randy right from balls to tip),

Fucking or sucking, there's a twist
You give your arse – and what a gift! –
That decent ladies have all missed:
By God, you've reason in that rift!

And when we kiss, your tongue takes on
Such long and penetrating parts
So ardently that (shit!) it's gone
Straight down into my heart of hearts,

And your quim drains my white liqueur
As a bear milks its mother's dug –
A cub well-licked, with such rich fur
My own rolls on it for a rug:

Licked into shape – my tongue, old soak
And glutton, swears it's long lost count
Of hours spent playing, stroke by stroke,
The cough-sweet game beneath the Mount:

Well-licked, yes – bitter, though, and grim
That red laugh cut in your brown skin,
Your pretty, teasing, cheeky quim:
So like the lips of Harlequin.

PAUL VERLAINE
translated by Alistair Elliot

[90]

Put a Finger up My Arse, You Dear Old Man

Put a finger up my arse, you dear old man,
And push your tool in through the hairy hall;
Lift this leg good and high, and have a ball,
Ringing the changes though – not all can-can!

Faith, that's the stuff to get between your teeth –
Better than bread and dripping by the fire –
And if the cunt puts no juice in your wire,
Change sockets: you're all buggers, underneath.

This time I'll do your cunt, if that suits you;
And next time up both cunt and arse my tool
Will make us happy – and you holy too.

Anyone with ambitions is a fool.
Who wants to run the world? – if not to screw,
What are days for? To sleep, to make nights naughtier!

Let Castiglione's Courtier
Die in a palace waiting to inherit:
I only want to exercise the ferret.

PIETRO ARETINO
translated by Alistair Elliot

John Anderson, My Jo

John Anderson, my jo, John,
  I wonder what ye mean,
To lie sae lang i' the mornin',
  And sit sae late at e'en?
Ye'll bleer a' your een, John,
  And why do ye so?
Come sooner to your bed at e'en,
  John Anderson, my jo.

John Anderson, my jo, John,
  When first that ye began,
Ye had as good a tail-tree,
  As ony ither man;
But now it's waxen wan, John,
  And wrinkles to and fro;
I've twa gae-ups for ae gae-down,
  John Anderson, my jo.

I'm backit like a salmon,
  I'm breastit like a swan;
My wame it is a down-cod,
  My middle ye may span:
Frae my tap-knot to my tae, John,
  I'm like the new-fa'n snow;
And it's a' for your convenience,
  John Anderson, my jo.

O it is a fine thing
  To keep out o'er the dyke;
But it's a meikle finer thing,
  To see your hurdies fyke;
To see you hurdies fyke, John,
  And hit the rising blow;
It's then I like your chanter-pipe,
  John Anderson, my jo.

When ye come on before, John,
 See that ye do your best;
When ye begin to haud me,
 See that ye grip me fast;
See that ye grip me fast, John,
 Until that I cry 'Oh!'
Your back shall crack or I do that,
 John Anderson, my jo.

John Anderson, my jo, John,
 Ye're welcome when ye please;
It's either in the warm bed
 Or else aboon the claes:
Or ye shall hae the horns, John,
 Upon your head to grow;
An' that's the cuckold's mallison,
 John Anderson, my jo.

ROBERT BURNS

Wimbledon Veteran

In the shadow of a stand
You're waiting to receive;
To take my service.
You're set up,
But I'm forty, love.
Can I keep it up?
New balls, please!

LAWRENCE SUTTON

The Disabled Debauchee

As some brave admiral in former war,
Deprived of force, but pressed with courage still,
Two rival fleets appearing from afar,
Crawls to the top of some adjacent hill:

From whence (with thoughts full of concern) he views
The wise and daring conduct of the fight,
And each bold action to his mind renews
His present glory and his past delight;

From his fierce eyes flashes of rage he throws,
As from black clouds when lightning breaks away,
Transported, thinks himself amidst his foes,
And absent, yet enjoys the bloody day;

So when my days of impotence approach,
And I'm pox and wine's unlucky chance
Forced from the pleasing billows of debauch
On the dull shore of lazy temperance,

My pains at least some respite shall afford,
Whilst I behold the battles you maintain,
When fleets of glasses sail about the board,
From whose broadsides volleys of wit shall rain.

Nor let the sight of honourable scars
Which my too forward valour did procure,
Frighten new-listed soldiers from the wars;
Past joys have more than paid what I endure.

Should any youth (worth being drunk) prove nice,
And from his fair inviter meanly shrink,
'Twill please the ghost of my departed vice
If, at my counsel, he repent and drink.

Or should some cold-complexioned sot forbid
With his dull morals our night's brisk alarms,
I'll fire his blood by telling what I did
When I was strong and able to bear arms.

I'll tell of whores attacked, their lords at home,
Bawds' quarters beaten up and fortress won,
Windows demolished, watches overcome
And handsome ills by my contrivance done.

Nor shall our love-fits, Chloris, be forgot,
When each the well-looked link-boy strove to enjoy,
And the best kiss was the deciding lot,
Whether the boy fucked you, or I the boy.

With tales like these I will such thoughts inspire,
As to important mischief shall incline.
I'll make him long some ancient church to fire
And fear no lewdness he's called to by wine.

Thus, statesmanlike, I'll saucily impose,
And, safe from action, valiantly advise,
Sheltered in impotence urge you to blows
And, being good for nothing else, be wise.

JOHN WILMOT, EARL OF ROCHESTER

Endpiece

Here lies the body of Patrick
Who served Aphrodite delightedly.
Even when quite geriatric
He still raised a nightie excitedly.

PATRICK O'SHAUGHNESSY

IT CERTAINLY IS

Circe

It certainly is the smell of her cunt
makes you fall on your knees and grunt.

It certainly is the slope of her tits
makes your morality fall to bits.

It certainly is her incurved waist
makes you long for that truffle taste.

It certainly is her pubic thighs
makes your piglike prick uprise.

It certainly is her heavenly hair
makes you wallow and keeps you bare.

It certainly is her beautiful bum
makes you rootle and holds you dumb.

It certainly is her feminine hands
makes you the slave of glorious glands.

It certainly is the commanding eye
makes you happy to live in a sty.

GAVIN EWART

A Ballad of the Good Lord Nelson

The Good Lord Nelson had a swollen gland,
Little of the scripture did he understand
Till a woman led him to the promised land
   Aboard the Victory, Victory O.

Adam and Eve and a bushel of figs
Meant nothing to Nelson who was keeping pigs,
Till a woman showed him the various rigs
   Aboard the Victory, Victory O.

His heart was softer than a new-laid egg,
Too poor for loving and ashamed to beg,
Till Nelson was taken by the Dancing Leg
   Aboard the Victory, Victory O.

Now he up and did up his little tin trunk
And he took to the ocean on his English junk,
Turning like the hour-glass in his lonely bunk
   Aboard the Victory, Victory O.

The Frenchman saw him a-coming there
With the one-piece eye and the valentine hair.
With the safety-pin sleeve and occupied air
   Aboard the Victory, Victory O.

Now you all remember the message he sent
As an answer to Hamilton's discontent –
There were questions asked about it in Parliament
   Aboard the Victory, Victory O.

Now the blacker the berry, the thicker comes the juice.
Think of Good Lord Nelson and avoid self-abuse,
For the empty sleeve was no mere excuse
   Aboard the Victory, Victory O.

'England Expects' was the motto he gave
When he thought of little Emma out on Biscay's wave,
And remembered working on her like a galley-slave
   Aboard the Victory, Victory O.

The finest Great Lord in our English land
To honour the Freudian command,
For a cast in the bush is worth two in the hand
   Aboard the Victory, Victory O.

Now the Frenchman shot him there as he stood
In the rage of battle in a silk-lined hood
And he heard the whistle of his own hot blood
   Aboard the Victory, Victory O.

Now stiff on a pillar with a phallic air
Nelson stylites in Trafalgar Square
Reminds the British what once they were
   Aboard the Victory, Victory O.

If they'd treat their women in the Nelson way
There'd be fewer frigid husbands every day
And many more heroes on the Bay of Biscay
   Aboard the Victory, Victory O.

       LAWRENCE DURRELL

Prelude

It wouldn't be a good idea
To let him stay.
When they knew each other better –
Not today.
But she put on her new black knickers
Anyway.

WENDY COPE

Pendydd

Love is like butter, Evans mused, and stuck
The last pat on his toast. Breakfast in bed
At the Red Dragon – when Miss Protheroe,
Wearing her weekday suit, had caught the train
Back home, or rather to her place of work,
United Mutual Trust – encouraged thought,
And so did the try-asking-me-then look
The bird who fetched the food had given him.
Scrub that for now. Love is like butter. It
Costs money but, fair play, not all that much,
However hard you go at it there's more,
Though to have nothing else would turn you up
(Like those two fellows on that raft,* was it?),
Nothing spreads thinner when you're running short;
Natural? Well, yes and no. Better than guns,
And – never mind what the heart experts say –
Let's face it, bloody good for you. Dead odd
That two things should turn out so much alike,
He thought, ringing the bell for more of both.

KINGSLEY AMIS

*Dinghy, actually. Evans is thinking of an episode in *The Bombard Story* (Penguin edn., p. 17). [K.A.]

from The Zeg-Zeg Postcards

I

Africa – London – Africa –
to get it away.

II

My white shorts tighten
in the market crowds.
I don't know
if a lean Fulani boy
or girl gave me this stand
trailing his/her knuckles
on my thigh.

III

Knowing my sense of ceremonial
my native tailor
still puts
buttons on my flies.

IV

I bought three *Players* tins
of groundnuts with green mould
just to touch your hand
counting the coppers into mine.

V

My Easter weekend Shangri-la, Pankshin.
I watch you pour the pure
well water, balanced up the mountain,
in blinding kerosene cans,
each lovely morning, convict,
your release date, nineteen years from now,
daubed in brown ink on your rotting shirt.

VI

My *White Horse* plastic horses carousel
whirls round an empty and my hell,
when the last neat whisky passes my cracked lips,
is a riderless Apocalypse.

VII *Water Babies*

She hauls at his member like a crude *shaduf*
to give her dry loins life, and calls it love.

She's back in England pregnant. Now he can
flood the damned valley of his African.

VIII

Sex beefs at belled virginity. The wives
nag back at sex. Ding, Dong! Ding, Dong!
rings no changes on their married lives
clapping out *Love's Old Sweet Song*.

What's that to me? I can get a stand
even from maps of the Holy Land.

IX

Je suis le ténébreux . . . le veuf . . .
always the *soixante* and never the *neuf.*

X

It's time for tea and biscuits. No one comes.
I hear the flap of Dunlop sandals, drums,
terrifying cries. My clap still bothers me.
Siestas make me dizzy. I stagger up and see
through mesh and acacia sharp metal flash,
my steward, still in white uniform and sash,
waving a sharpened piece of Chevie, ride
his old *Raleigh* to the genocide.

XI

The shower streams over him
and the water turns instantly
to cool *Coca-Cola.*

XII

We shake baby powder over each other
like men salting a spitroast,
laughing like kids in a sandpit,
childish ghosts of ourselves,
me, puffy marshmallow, he,
sherbet-dusted liquorice
licked back bright
and leading into *Turkish Delight.*

XIII

Buttocks. Buttocks.
You pronounce it as though
the syllables rhymed: *loo*; *cocks*.
I murmur over and over:
buttocks . . . buttocks . . . BUTOX,
marketable essence of beef –
négritude – dilute to taste!

XIV

I'd like to
sukuru
you.

XV

Mon égal!
Let me be the Gambia
in your Senegal.

TONY HARRISON

I Sometimes Think

This couplet was attributed to John Betjeman (with assistance from W. H. Auden and Louis MacNeice, an unlikely triad) on p. 258 of *Young Betjeman* by Bevis Hillier (John Murray, 1988). I have since learned from John Murray that this attribution is erroneous. Anon. it is, therefore.

I sometimes think that I should like
To be the saddle of a bike.

ANON.

Grease

Grease steals in like a lover
over the body of my oven.
Grease kisses the knobs
of my stove.
Grease plays with the small
hands of my spoons.
Grease caresses the skin
of my table-cloth,
Getting into every crease.
Grease reassures me that life
is naturally sticky.

Grease is obviously having an affair with me.

GRACE NICHOLS

Dearest Ipsitilla

Dearest Ipsitilla, I'd absolutely love it,
my darling girl, my gorgeous smarty-pants –
do send for me to come . . . this afternoon.
And when you do, it would be very helpful if
you'd please ensure that no one's barred the way
to your front door, and you're *at home*: don't you
slip off! Stay put, and get things ready for
our feast of nine successive inter-courses!
You really want some action? Ask me *now*!
I'm stuffed with breakfast, all stretched out, and you
should see my banger blasting through the sheets!

CATULLUS
translated by Rodney Pybus

In Summer's Heat

In summer's heat and mid-time of the day,
To rest my limbs upon a bed a lay,
One window shut, the other open stood,
Which gave such light as twinkles in a wood
Like twilight glimpse at setting of the sun,
Or night being past and yet not day begun.
Such light to shamefaced maidens must be shown,
Where they may sport, and seem to be unknown.
Then came Corinna in a long, loose gown,
Her white neck hid with tresses hanging down,
Resembling fair Semiramis going to bed,
Or Lais of a thousand wooers sped.
I snatched her gown, being thin the harm was small,
Yet strived she to be covered therewithal,
And, striving thus as one that would be chaste,
Betrayed herself, and yielded at the last.
Stark naked as she stood before mine eye,
Not one wen in her body could I spy.
What arms and shoulders did I touch and see?
How apt her breasts were to be pressed by me?
How smooth a belly under her waist saw I?
How large a leg, and what a lusty thigh?
To leave the rest, all liked me passing well;
I clinged her naked body, down she fell.
Judge you the rest. Being tired, she bade me kiss.
Jove send me more such afternoons as this.

OVID
translated by Christopher Marlowe

Rural Rides: The Tractor Driver

When the tractor driver's ride is bumpy
He grits his teeth and thinks of scrumpy,
And that Dorset wench with winsome dimples
Who lives in Weymouth and has big Bristols.

ROBERT MAITRE

Idyll 27

Daphnis The shepherd Paris bore the Spartan bride
           By force away, and then by force enjoyed;
           But I by free consent can boast a bliss,
           A fairer Helen, and a sweeter kiss.
Chloris Kisses are empty joys and soon are o'er.
Daphnis A kiss betwixt the lips is something more.
Chloris I wipe my mouth, and where's your kissing then?
Daphnis I swear you wipe it to be kissed again.
Chloris Go tend your herd, and kiss your cows at home;
           I am a maid, and in my beauty's bloom.
Daphnis 'Tis well remembered, do not waste your time;
           But wisely use it ere you pass your prime.
Chloris Blown roses hold their sweetness to the last,
           And raisins keep their luscious native taste.
Daphnis The sun's too hot; these olive shades are near;
           I fain would whisper something in your ear.
Chloris 'Tis honest talking where we may be seen,
           God knows that secret mischief you may mean;
           I doubt you'll play the wag and kiss again.
Daphnis At least beneath yon elm you need not fear;
           My pipe's in tune, if you're disposed to hear.
Chloris Play by yourself, I dare not venture thither:
           You, and your naughty pipe go hang together.
Daphnis Coy nymph beware, lest Venus you offend.
Chloris I shall have chaste Diana still to friend.
Daphnis You have a soul, and Cupid has a dart.
Chloris Diana will defend, or heal my heart.
           Nay, fie what mean you in this open place?
           Unhand me, or, I swear, I'll scratch your face.
           Let go for shame; you make me mad for spite;
           My mouth's my own; and if you kiss I'll bite.
Daphnis Away with your dissembling female tricks:
           What, would you 'scape the fate of all your sex?

Chloris   I swear I'll keep my maidenhead till death,
And die as pure as Queen Elizabeth.

Daphnis   Nay mum for that; but let me lay thee down;
Better with me, than with some nauseous clown.

Chloris   I'd have you know, if I were so inclined,
I have been wooed by many a wealthy hind;
But never found a husband to my mind.

Daphnis   But they are absent all; and I am here.

Chloris   The matrimonial yoke is hard to bear;
And marriage is a woeful word to hear.

Daphnis   A scarecrow, set to frighten fools away;
Marriage has joys; and you shall have a say.

Chloris   Sour sauce is often mixed with our delight,
You kick by day more than you kiss by night.

Daphnis   Sham stories all; but say the worst you can,
A very wife fears neither God nor Man.

Chloris   But childbirth is they say, a deadly pain;
It costs at least a month to knit again.

Daphnis   Diana cures the wounds Lucina made;
Your goddess is a midwife by her trade.

Chloris   But I shall spoil my beauty if I bear.

Daphnis   But Mam and Dad are pretty names to hear.

Chloris   But there's a civil question used of late;
Where lies my jointure, where your own estate?

Daphnis   My flocks, my fields, my wood, my pastures take,
With settlement as good as law can make.

Chloris   Swear then you will not leave me on the common,
But marry me, and make an honest woman.

Daphnis   I swear by Pan (though he wears horns you'll say)
Cudgelled and kicked, I'll not be forced away.

Chloris   I bargain for a wedding bed at least,
A house, and handsome lodging for a guest.

Daphnis   A house well furnished shall be thine to keep;
And for a flock-bed I can shear my sheep.

Chloris   What tale shall I to my old father tell?

Daphnis   'Twill make him chuckle thou'rt bestowed so well.

Chloris   But after all, in troth I am to blame
          To be so loving ere I know your name.
          A pleasant-sounding name's a pretty thing.
Daphnis Faith, mine's a very pretty name to sing;
          They call me Daphnis: Lycidas my sire,
          Nomaea bore me; farmers in degree,
          He a good husband, a good housewife she.
Chloris   Your kindred is not much amiss, 'tis true,
          Yet I am somewhat better born than you.
Daphnis I know your father, and his family;
          And without boasting am as good as he:
          Menalcas; and no master goes before.
Chloris   Hang both our pedigrees; not one word more;
          But if you love me let me see your living,
          Your house and home; for seeing in believing.
Daphnis See first yon cypress grove, (a shade from noon).
Chloris   Browse on my goats; for I'll be with you soon.
Daphnis Feed well my bulls, to whet your appetite;
          That each may take a lusty leap at night.
Chloris   What do you mean (uncivil as you are),
          To touch my breasts, and leave my bosom bare?
Daphnis These pretty bubbies first I make my own.
Chloris   Pull out your hand, I swear, or I shall swoon.
Daphnis Why does the ebbing blood forsake thy face?
Chloris   Throw me at least upon a cleaner place:
          My linen ruffled, and my waistcoat soiling,
          What, do you think new clothes were made for
             spoiling?
Daphnis I'll lay me lambskins underneath thy back.
Chloris   My headgear's off; what filthy work you make!
Daphnis To Venus first, I lay these offerings by.
Chloris   Nay first look round, that nobody be nigh:
          Methinks I hear a whispering in the grove.
Daphnis The cypress trees are telling tales of love.
Chloris   You tear off all behind me, and before me;
          And I'm as naked as my mother bore me.

Daphnis I'll buy thee better clothes than these I tear,
         And lie so close, I'll cover thee from air.
Chloris Y'are liberal now; but when your turn is sped,
         You'll wish me choked with every crust of bread.
Daphnis I'll give thee more, much more than I have told;
         Would I could coin my very heart to gold.
Chloris Forgive thy handmaid (huntress of the wood),
         I see there's no resisting flesh and blood!
Daphnis The noble deed is done; my herds I'll cull;
         Cupid, be thine a calf; and Venus, thine a bull.
Chloris A maid I came, in an unlucky hour,
         But hence return, without my virgin flower.
Daphnis A maid is but a barren name at best;
         If thou canst hold, I bid for twins at least.

    Thus did this happy pair their love dispense
With mutual joys, and gratified their sense;
The god of love was there a bidden guest;
And present at his own mysterious feast.
His azure mantle underneath he spread,
And scattered roses on the nuptial bed;
While folded in each other's arms they lay,
He blew the flames, and furnished out the play,
And from their foreheads wiped the balmy sweat
    away.
First rose the maid and with a glowing face,
Her downcast eyes beheld her print upon the
    grass;
Thence to her herd she sped herself in haste:
The bridegroom started from his trance at last,
And piping homeward jocundly he passed.

                    THEOCRITUS
             translated by John Dryden

Some People

Some people like sex more than others –
You seem to like it a lot.
There's nothing wrong with being innocent or high-minded
But I'm glad you're not.

WENDY COPE

Let's Fuck, Dear Heart

Let's fuck, dear heart, let's have it in and out,
For we're obliged to fuck for being born,
And as I crave for cunt, you ache for horn,
Because the world would not make sense without.

If after death it were decent to be had,
I'd say: Let's fuck, let's fuck so much we die;
There we'll all fuck – you, Adam, Eve, and I –
For they invented death and thought it bad.

Really it's true that if those first two thieves
Had never eaten that perfidious fruit,
We'd still know how to fuck (though not wear leaves).

But no more gossip now; let's aim and shoot
The prick right to the heart, and make the soul
Burst as it dies in concert with the root.

And could your generous hole
Take in as witnesses these bobbing buoys
For inside testimony of our joys?

PIETRO ARETINO
translated by Alistair Elliot

To His Mistress Going to Bed

Come, Madam, come, all rest my powers defy,
Until I labour, I in labour lie.
The foe oft-times having the foe in sight,
Is tired with standing though they never fight.
Off with that girdle, like heaven's zone glistering,
But a far fairer world encompassing.
Unpin that 'spangled' breastplate which you wear,
That th' eyes of busy fools may be stopped there.
Unlace yourself, for that harmonious chime
Tells me from you, that now 'tis your bed time.
Off with that happy busk, which I envy,
That still can be, and still can stand so nigh.
Your gown going off, such beauteous state reveals,
As when from flowery meads th' hill's shadow steals.
Off with that wiry coronet and show
The hairy diadem which on you doth grow;
Now off with those shoes, and then safely tread
In this love's hallowed temple, this soft bed.
In such white robes heaven's angels used to be
Received by men; thou angel bring'st with thee
A heaven like Mahomet's paradise; and though
Ill spirits walk in white, we easily know
By this these angels from an evil sprite,
Those set our hairs, but these our flesh upright.
  Licence my roving hands, and let them go
Before, behind, between, above, below.
O my America, my new found land,
My kingdom, safeliest when with one man manned,
My mine of precious stones, my empery,
How blessed am I in this discovering thee!
To enter in these bonds, is to be free;
Then where my hand is set, my seal shall be.
  Full nakedness, all joys are due to thee.
As souls unbodied, bodies unclothed must be,

To taste whole joys. Gems which you women use
Are like Atlanta's balls, cast in men's views,
That when a fool's eye lighteth on a gem,
His earthly soul may covet theirs, not them.
Like pictures, or like books' gay coverings made
For laymen, are all women thus arrayed;
Themselves are mystic books, which only we
Whom their imputed grace will dignify
Must see revealed. Then since I may know,
As liberally, as to a midwife, show
Thyself: cast all, yea, this white linen hence,
Here is no penance, much less innocence.
    To teach thee, I am naked first, why then
What needst thou have more covering than a man.

JOHN DONNE

What Lips My Lips Have Kissed

What lips my lips have kissed, and where, and why,
I have forgotten, and what arms have lain
Under my head till morning; but the rain
Is full of ghosts tonight, that tap and sigh
Upon the glass and listen for reply,
And in my heart there stirs a quiet pain
For unremembered lads that not again
Will turn to me at midnight with a cry.
Thus in the winter stands the lonely tree,
Nor knows what birds have vanished one by one,
Yet knows its boughs more silent than before:
I cannot say what loves have come and gone,
I only know that summer sang in me
A little while, that in me sings no more.

EDNA ST VINCENT MILLAY

A Thousand and Three

My lovers come, not from the floating classes: they're
Labourers from the depths of suburbs or the land,
Aged fifteen, twenty, with no graces, but an air
Of pretty brutal strength and manners none too grand.

I like them in their work-clothes – jacket, overalls:
Smelling of pure and simple health, never a whiff
Of scent: their step sounds heavy, yes, but still it falls
Nimbly enough – they're young, their bounce a little stiff.

Their crafty and wide eyes crackle with cordial
Mischief: the wit of their naïvely knowing quips
Comes salted with gay swearwords, to be rhythmical,
From their fresh, wholesome mouths and soundly kissing
    lips;

With energetic knobs and buttockfuls of joy
They can rejoice my arsehole and my cock all night;
By lamplight and at dawn their flesh, all over joy,
Wakes my desire again, tired but still full of fight.

Thighs, hands, and souls, all of me mixed up, memory, feet,
Heart, back and ear and nose and all my ringing guts
Begin to bawl in chorus as they hit the beat,
Reeling and jig-a-jigging in their frenzied ruts:

A crazy dance, a crazy chorus as we're lined
Up, up, divinely rising because hell is high
On heavenly routes: I dance to save myself, and find,
Swimming in sweat, it's in our common breath I fly.

So, my two Charleses: one, young tiger with cat's eyes,
A choirboy with his volume swelling rough and thick;
The other a wild blade so cheeky I surprise
Him only with my dizzy penchant for his prick;

And Odilon, a kid, equipped, though, like a lord:
His feet in love with mine, which rave about their catch —
Those toes! — though thick and fast the rest of him's
    adored —
Those feet! — there's nothing like them! — even they don't
    match!

How they caress, so satin cool, with sensitive
Knuckles that stroke the soles and, round the ankles, graze
Over the veiny arch! how these strange kisses give
A sweet soul to this quadruped with soulful ways!

Then Antoine, with that tail of legendary size,
My god, my phallocrat who triumphs from the rear,
Piercing my heart with the blue lightning of his eyes,
My violet arsehole with his terrifying spear;

Paul, a blond athlete — pectorals that you could eat! —
A white breast with hard buttons that are sucked as much
As the more juicy end; and François, lithe as wheat,
His pecker coiled in that fantasic dancer's crutch;

Auguste, who daily makes himself more masculine
(Oh when it happened first he was a pretty lass!);
Jules, rather whorish with his pallid beauty's skin;
Henri, the marvellous conscript who's gone off, alas! —

I see you all, alone or friends together, some
Unique, some I confuse, a vision of past love
Clear as my passions who come now, or are to come,
My countless darlings who can never come enough!

PAUL VERLAINE
translated by Alistair Elliot

Green Grow the Rashes

O wat ye ought o fisher Meg,
   And how she trow'd the webster, O;
She loot me see her carrot cunt,
   And sell'd it for a labster, O.
     Green grow the rashes, O
       Green grow the rashes, O;
    The lassies they hae wimble-bores,
       The widows they hae gashes, O.

Mistress Mary cow'd her thing
   Because she wad be gentle, O
And span the fleece upon a rock
   To waft a highland mantle, O.
    Green grow, etc.

An' heard ye o the coat o arms
   The Lyon brought our lady, O?
The crest was couchant sable cunt,
   The motto *ready, ready*, O.
    Green grow, etc.

An' ken ye Leezie Lundie, O,
   The godly Leezie Lundie, O?
She mows like reek thro a' the week,
   But finger-fucks on Sunday, O.
    Green grow, etc.

     ROBERT BURNS

Sappho to Philaenis

Where is that holy fire, which verse is said
   To have? is that enchanting force decayed?
Verse, that draws Nature's works, from Nature's law,
   Thee, her best work, to her work cannot draw.
Have my tears quenched my old poetic fire;
   Why quenched they not as well, that of desire?
Thoughts, my mind's creatures, often are with thee,
   But I, their maker, want their liberty.
Only thine image, in my heart, doth sit,
   But that is wax, and fires environ it.
My fires have driven, thine have drawn it hence;
   And I am robbed of picture, heart, and sense.
Dwells with me still mine irksome memory,
   Which, both to keep, and lose, grieves equally.
That tells me how fair thou art: thou art so fair,
   As, gods, when gods to thee I do compare,
Are graced thereby; and to make blind men see,
   What things gods are, I say they are like to thee.
For, if we justly call each silly man
   A little world, what shall we call thee then?
Thou art not soft, and clear, and straight, and fair,
   As down, as stars, cedars, and lilies are,
But thy right hand, and cheek, and eye, only
   Are like thy other hand, and cheek, and eye.
Such was my Phao awhile, but shall be never,
   As thou wast, art, and, oh, mayst thou be ever.
Here lovers swear in their idolatry,
   That I am such; but grief discolours me.
And yet I grieve the less, lest grief remove
   My beauty, and make me unworthy of thy love.
Plays some soft boy with thee, oh there wants yet
   A mutual feeling which should sweeten it.
His chin, a thorny hairy unevenness
   Doth threaten, and some daily change possess.

[127]

Thy body is a natural paradise,
   In whose self, unmanured, all pleasure lies,
Nor needs perfection; why shouldst thou then
   Admit the tillage of a harsh rough man?
Men leave behind them that which their sin shows,
   And are as thieves traced, which rob when it snows.
But of our dalliance no more signs there are,
   Than fishes leave in streams, or birds in air.
And between us all sweetness may be had;
   All, all that Nature yields, or Art can add.
My two lips, eyes, thighs, differ from thy two,
   But so, as thine from one another do;
And, oh, no more; the likeness being such,
   Why should they not alike in all parts touch?
Hand to strange hand, lip to lip none denies;
   Why should they breast to breast, or thighs to thighs?
Likeness begets such strange self-flattery,
   That touching myself, all seems done to thee.
Myself I embrace, and mine own hands I kiss,
   And amorously thank myself for this.
Me, in my glass, I call thee; but alas,
   When I would kiss, tears dim mine eyes, and glass.
O cure this loving madness, and restore
   Me to me; thee, my half, my all, my more.
So may thy cheeks' red outwear scarlet dye,
   And their white, whiteness of the galaxy,
So may thy mighty, amazing beauty move
   Envy in all women, and in all men, love,
And so be change, and sickness, far from thee,
   As thou by coming near, keep'st them from me.

JOHN DONNE

from Love, Death and the Changing of the Seasons

First, I want to make you come in my hand
while I watch you and kiss you, and if you cry,
I'll drink your tears while, with my whole hand, I
hold your drenched loveliness contracting. And
after a breath, I want to make you full
again, and wet. I want to make you come
in my mouth like a storm. No tears now. The sum
of your parts is my whole most beautiful
chart of the constellations – your left breast
in my mouth again. You know you'll have to be
your age. As I lie beside you, cover me
like a gold cloud, hands everywhere, at last
inside me where I trust you, then your tongue
where I need you. I want you to make me come.

MARILYN HACKER

My Legs Half Round Your Neck

My legs half round your neck, and with your cock
Plugged in my arse, I find myself shoved head-
first on the clothes-chest, off the clattering bed.
What pleasure's this you're adding to my stock?
Get me back on the bed, I'll break in two
Hung upside-down over the edge like this.
Shit! in comparison, bearing kids was bliss.
Cruel love, dear god, what have you brought me to?

   – Well, what have you in mind then?
                  – What you like:
Give us your tongue a little, come, dear soul,
To serve in silence is to ask a lot:

Post me some pleasure in the vital slot,
Else there'll be no peace between hole and hole.
Push, friend: the damn cock's sliding off on strike!

      Sure it would kill me if I'd got
Much more to wait for the relief of pleasure
From you, my favourite thing, my heart, my treasure.

PIETRO ARETINO
translated by Alistair Elliot

Hetero-sex is Best

Hetero-sex is best for the man of a serious turn of mind,
But here's a hint, if you should fancy the other:
Turn Menophila round in bed, address her peachy behind,
And it's easy to pretend you're screwing her brother.

MARCUS ARGENTARIUS
translated by Fleur Adcock

If You See Someone

If you see someone beautiful
    hammer it out right then.
Say what you think; put your hands full
    on his bollocks: be a man.

But if 'I admire you' is what you say
    and 'I'll be a brother to you' –
shame will bar the only way
    to all you want to do.

ADAIOS
translated by Alistair Elliot

Don't

Don't squash your arse against the wall.
Them stones are good for bugger all.

STRATO
translated by Fergus Pickering

The Miracle

'Right to the end, that man, he was so hot
That driving to the airport we stopped off
At some McDonald's and do you know what,
We did it there. He couldn't get enough.'
– 'There at the counter?' – 'No, that's public stuff:

'There in the rest room. He pulled down my fly,
And through his shirt I felt him warm and trim.
I squeezed his nipples and began to cry
At losing this, my miracle, so slim
That I could grip my wrist in back of him.

'Then suddenly he dropped down on one knee
Right by the urinal in his only suit
And let it fly, saying Keep it there for me,
And smiling up. I can still see him shoot.
Look at that snail-track on the toe of my boot.'

– 'Snail-track?' – 'Yes, there.' – 'That was six months ago.
How can it still be there?' – 'My friend, at night
I make it shine again, I love him so,
Like they renew a saint's blood out of sight.
But we're not Catholic, see, so it's all right.'

THOM GUNN

Sexual Couplets

Here we are, without our clothes,
one excited watering can, one peculiar rose . . .

My shoe-tree wants to come,
and stretch your body where it lies undone . . .

I am wearing a shiny sou'wester;
you are coxcombed like a jester . . .

Oh my strangely gutted one,
the fish head needs your flesh around its bone . . .

We move in anapaestic time and pause,
until my body rhymes with yours . . .

In the valley of your arse,
all flesh is grass, all flesh is grass . . .

One damp acorn on the tweedy sod –
then the broad bean dangles in its pod . . .

CRAIG RAINE

Rim of Red

'She rode a race on me,' Jim chauffeur said
'She took her specs off and her tits fair swung.'

They were the days they bought french letters coiled
In mock cigarettes. 'Bloody near drew it off

Of me.' He and I lay naked beside the cold Test
And with affection he stroked his cock.

Nobody else on the river bank. 'I'll get a horn
On it if we don't go in again.' I was ten.

'Those bleeding fish worth a thousand quid a mile a week.'
With rushing weeds and cold that already hurt.

But often naked by rivers or seas I have
remembered my idea of how her nose would bear

A rim of red from steel glasses, breasts like swings.
And confiding, white, hairy Jim, favouring his cock.

BERNARD GUTTERIDGE

A Fragment of Petronius Arbiter

Doing, a filthy pleasure is, and short;
And done, we straight repent us of the sport:
Let us not then rush blindly on unto it,
Like lustful beasts, that only know how to do it:
For lust will languish, and that heat decay.
But thus, thus, keeping endless Holy-day,
Let us together closely lie, and kiss,
There is no labour, nor no shame in this;
This hath pleased, doth please, and long will please; never
Can this decay, but is beginning ever.

?PETRONIUS
translated by Ben Jonson

ON THE ROCKS

Two Sonnets *from On the Rocks*

Fuck the gossip. Fuck the backstabbing. Fuck the
Contumelious, pusillanimous, parasitic, spitting, confidante.
Fuck the broken windows, the dripping gutters. Fuck the
Bills, the future, the holes in my socks, the elephant
Crashing around in my memory. Fuck the odour
Of forgiveness, the nice little boy philosophy.
And fuck that nice little boy you picked up in the bar
Down by the river. Fuck him. Fuck him. And fuck the
    private eye
On our public adoration. Fuck the lot of them.
And fuck those friends, the ones who helped to screw us
With soft chat to the very joists of heaven.
Fuck alcohol. Fuck cigarettes. And fuck the smell of
    hashish.
Fuck everything in fact. In fact, fuck
Me, you cunt. Yes, me. If you're in luck.

Why you triple-headed cunt, no wonder you wanted a
    separation.
Your conscience got a little hot. You wanted to cool off.
(One for him, one for me, and one for the relation-
Ship with your doctor). You are not nearly as tough
As you think, in your almighty beauty, you must be.
You have forgotten the law of cause and effect. The law
Of laws. The fact that if you spill a glass of whisky
In Montreal, a match gets struck in midnight Arkansas.
So there you were, stealing the fond embrace,
The lavatory kiss, feeling the itch for his balls
Even in our living room, while I grew blind in my place,
My grovelling place, I here abjure with your fucking pills.
And you snucked right off to our bedroom,
Cunt awash, orgiastic with that twit, giggling in our new
    home.

SEBASTIAN BARKER

Kisses Loathsome

I abhor the slimy kiss,
(Which to me most loathsome is).
Those lips please me which are placed
Close, but not too strictly laced:
Yielding I would have them; yet
Not a wimbling tongue admit:
What would poking sticks make there,
When the ruff is set elsewhere?

ROBERT HERRICK

from The Choice of Valentines

'Oh not so fast,' my ravished mistress cries,
'Lest my content, than on thy life relies
Be brought too soon from his delightful seat,
And me unawares of hoped bliss defeat.
Together let our equal motions stir,
Together let us live and die my dear,
Together let us march unto content,
And be consumed with one blandishment.'
As she prescribed, so kept we crotchet-time,
And every stroke in order like a chime.
Whilst she, that had preserved me by her pity,
Unto our music framed a groaning ditty.
Alas, alas, that love should be a sin,
Even now my bliss and sorrow doeth begin.
Hold wide thy lap, my lovely Danaë,
And entertain the golden shower so free,
That trilling falls into thy treasury,
As April drops not half so pleasant be,
Nor Nilus overflow, to Egypt plains,
As this sweet stream, that all her joints embaynes;
With *Oh*, and *Oh*, she itching moves her hips,
And to and fro, full lightly starts and skips.
She jerks her legs, and sprawleth with her heels,
No tongue may tell the solace that she feels.
I faint, I yield; Oh death rock me asleep;
Sleep – sleep desire, entombed in the deep.
'Not so my dear,' my dearest saint replied;
'For, from us yet thy spirit may not glide
Until the sinewy channels of our blood
Withhold their source from this imprisoned flood;
And then will we (that then will come too soon)
Dissolved lie as though our days were done.
The whilst I speak, my soul is fleeting hence,
And life forsakes his fleshy residence.

Stay, stay sweet joy, and leave me not forlorn,
Why shouldst thou fade, that art but newly born?
Stay but an hour; an hour is not so much,
But half an hour; if that thy haste be such:
Nay but a quarter; I will ask no more,
That thy departure (which torments me sore)
May be alightened with a little pause,
And take away this passion's sudden cause.
He hears me not, hard-hearted as he is:
He is the son of Time, and hates my bliss.
Time ne'er looks back, the rivers ne'er return;
A second spring must help me or I burn.'
'No, no, the well is dry that should refresh me,
The glass is run of all my destiny.
Nature of winter learneth nigardise,
Who, as he overbears the stream with ice,
That man nor beast may of their pleasance taste,
So shuts she up her conduit all in haste,
And will not let her nectar overflow,
Lest mortal men immortal joys should know.'
'Adieu unconstant love, to thy disport,
Adieu false mirth, and melody too-short.
Adieu faint-hearted instrument of lust,
That falsely hast betrayed our equal trust.
Henceforth no more will I implore thine aid,
Or thee, or men of cowardice upbraid.
My little dildo shall supply their kind:
A knave, that moves as light as leaves by wind;
That bendeth not, nor foldeth any deal,
But stands as stiff, as he were made of steel,
And plays at peacock twixt my legs right blithe,
And doeth my tickling assuage with many a sigh;
For, by Saint Runnion he'll refresh me well,
And never make my tender belly swell.'

THOMAS NASHE

[144]

No Joke

'In respect of the recurrent emergence of the theme of sex . . . it must always be remembered that his locale was Celtic and his season spring.'
Judge John M. Woolsey, United States of America v. One Book called *Ulysses*, 6 December 1933.

A man's two people, well and sick,
nailed to the gallows of his prick.
Plead theft, or rape, or race, or spring.
Plead love. Plead any bloody thing.
Plead art, religion, tenderness,
provocation of a dress,
subtle spice, a Coptic cook,
the dialectic of a look.

No joke, no joke, the huge, despotic
orphanage of cunt and prick
doing solitary near
the borders of Illyria
where Poldy's Molly's Celtic brief
broke all the gallows into leaf.

WILLIAM SCAMMELL

the thing you'll like best

the thing you'll like best about going to bed with men
is their astonishing bigness.
even the little ones are bigger than us
yet they take care to fit.

the thing you'll like best about going to bed with men
is their pleasant politeness.
lips that would say ughnastyswampcunt
dip tastefully to kiss it.

the thing you'll like best about going to bed with men
is the featherbrush of hands like spanners
on anxious buttons; the way they don't
complain if service is long arriving.

the thing you'll like best about going to bed with men
is the vigour of the arms that hold you
not to imprison, not to lay waste,
but to encourage for some ordeal
where you'll prove you're not a witch by drowning.

the thing you'll like best about going to bed with men
is the sense of being let off.

ZOË FAIRBAIRNS

Song

Love a *woman*! You're an ass,
  'Tis a most insipid passion,
To choose out for your happiness
  The idlest part of God's creation!

Let the porter and the groom,
  Things designed for dirty slaves,
Drudge in fair Aurelia's womb,
  To get supplies for age and graves.

Farewell Woman. I intend,
  Henceforth, every night to sit
With my lewd, well-natured friend,
  Drinking, to engender wit.

Then give me Health, Wealth, Mirth and Wine,
  And if busy Love entrenches,
There's a sweet, soft page of mine
  Does the trick worth forty wenches.

JOHN WILMOT, EARL OF ROCHESTER

Either She was Foul

Either she was foul, or her attire was bad,
Or she was not the wench I wished t'have had.
Idly I lay with her, as if I loved not,
And like a burden grieved the bed that moved not.
Yet though both of us performed our true intent,
Yet could I not cast anchor where I meant.
She on my neck her ivory arms did throw,
Her arms far whiter than the Scythian snow.
And eagerly she kissed me with her tongue,
And under mine her wanton thigh she flung.
Yea, and she soothed me up and called me sire,
And used all speech that might provoke and stir.
Yet, like as if cold hemlock I had drunk,
It mockèd me, hung down the head, and sunk.
Like a dull cipher or rude block I lay,
Or shade or body was I, who can say?
What will my age do, age I cannot shun,
When in my prime my force is spent and done?
I blush, that being youthful, hot and lusty,
I prove neither youth nor man, but old and rusty.
Pure rose she, like a nun to sacrifice,
Or one that with her tender brother lies.
Yet boarded I the golden Chie twice,
And Libas, and the white-cheeked Pitho thrice.
Corinna craved it in a summer's night,
And nine sweet bouts we had before daylight.
What, waste my limbs through some Thessalian charms?
May spells and drugs do silly souls such harms?
With virgin wax hath some imbaste my joints
And pierced my liver with sharp needles' points?
Charms change corn to grass and make it die.
By charms are running springs and fountains dry.
By charms mast drops from oaks, from vines grapes fall,
And fruit from trees when there's no wind at all.

Why might not then my sinews be enchanted,
And I grow faint, as with some spirit haunted?
To this add shame: shame to perform it quailed me
And was the second cause why vigour failed me.
My idle thoughts delighted her no more
Than did the robe or garment which she wore.
Yet might her touch make youthful Pylius fire
And Tithon livelier than his years require.
Even her I had, and she had me in vain;
What might I crave more if I ask again?
I think the great gods grieved they had bestowed
The benefit which lewdly I for-slowed.
I wished to be received in. In I get me
To kiss. I kiss. To lie with her, she let me.
Why was I blessed? Why made king to refuse it?
Chuff-like had I not gold and could not use it?
So in a spring thrives he that told so much,
And looks upon the fruits he cannot touch.
Hath any rose so from a fresh young maid,
As she might straight have gone to church and prayed?
Well I believe she kissed not as she should,
Nor used the sleight and cunning which she could.
Huge oaks, hard adamants might she have moved,
And with sweet words cause deaf rocks to have loved.
Worthy she was to move both gods and men,
But neither was I man, nor lived then.
Can deaf ear take delight when Phaemius sings?
Or Thamiras in curious painted things?
What sweet thought is there but I had the same?
And one gave place still as another came.
Yet, nonwithstanding, like one dead it lay,
Drooping more than a rose pulled yesterday.
Now, when he should not jet, he bolts upright
And craves his task, and seeks to be at fight.
Lie down with shame, and see thou stir no more,
Seeing thou wouldst deceive me as before.

Thou cozenest me, by thee surprised am I,
And bide sore loss with endless infamy.
Nay more, the wench did not disdain a whit
To take it in her hand and play with it.
But when she saw it would by no means stand,
But still drooped down, regarding not her hand,
'Why mockst thou me?' she cried, 'Or, being ill,
Who bade thee lie down here against thy will?
Either thou art witch, with blood of frogs new dead,
Or jaded camest thou from some other bed.'
With that, her loose gown on, from me she cast her —
In skipping out her naked feet much graced her.
And, lest her maid should know of this disgrace,
To cover it, spilt water on the place.

OVID
translated by Christopher Marlowe

Beasts Copulate

Beasts copulate and are contented.
Man, by taking thought, invented
Buggery. The one who fucks
Is harking back to dogs and ducks.

STRATO
translated by Fergus Pickering

The Ballad of Villon and Fat Madge

''Tis no sin for a man to labour in his vocation.'
'The night cometh, when no man can work.'

What though the beauty I love and serve be cheap,
    Ought you to take me for a beast or fool?
All things a man could wish are in her keep;
    For her I turn swashbuckler in love's school.
    When folk drop in, I take my pot and stool
And fall to drinking with no more ado.
I fetch them bread, fruit, cheese, and water, too;
    I say all's right so long as I'm well paid;
'Look in again when your flesh troubles you,
    Inside this brothel where we drive our trade.'

But soon the devil's among us flesh and fell,
    When penniless to bed comes Madge my whore;
I loathe the very sight of her like hell.
    I snatch gown, girdle, surcoat, all she wore,
    And tell her, these shall stand against her score.
She grips her hips with both hands, cursing God,
Swearing by Jesus' body, bones, and blood,
    That they shall not. Then I, no whit dismayed,
Cross her cracked nose with some stray shiver of wood
    Inside this brothel where we drive our trade.

When all's up she drops me a windy word,
    Bloat like a beetle puffed and poisonous:
Grins, thumps my pate, and calls me dickey-bird,
    And cuffs me with a fist that's ponderous.
    We sleep like logs, being drunken both of us;
Then when we wake her womb begins to stir;
To save her seed she gets me under her
    Wheezing and whining, flat as planks are laid:
And thus she spoils me for a whoremonger
    Inside this brothel where we drive our trade.

Blow, hail or freeze, I've bread here baked rent free!
Whoring's my trade, and my whore pleases me;
  Bad cat, bad rat; we're just the same if weighed.
We that love filth, filth follows us, you see;
Honour flies from us, as from her we flee
  Inside this brothel where we drive our trade.

    I bequeath likewise to fat Madge
      This little song to learn and study;
    By God's head she's a sweet fat fadge,
      Devout and soft of flesh and ruddy;
    I love her with my soul and body,
    So doth she me, sweet dainty thing.
      If you fall in with such a lady,
    Read it, and give it her to sing.

          FRANÇOIS VILLON
translated by Algernon Charles Swinburne

Duncan Gray

Can ye play me *Duncan Gray*,
  Ha, ha, the girdin' o't;
O'er the hills an' far away,
  Ha, ha, the girdin' o't.
Duncan cam our Meg to woo,
Meg was nice an' wadna do,
But like an ither puff'd an' blew
  At offer o' the girdin' o't.

Duncan, he cam here again,
  Ha, ha, the girdin' o't,
A' was out an' Meg her lane,
  Ha, ha, the girdin' o't.
He kiss'd her butt, he kiss'd her ben,
He bang'd a thing against her wame –
But troth, I now forget its name
  But I trow she gat the girdin' o't.

She took him to the cellar then,
  Ha, ha, the girdin' o't,
To see gif he could do't again,
  Ha, ha, the girdin' o't.
He kiss'd her ance, he kiss'd her twice,
An' by the bye he kiss'd her thrice
Till deil a mair the thing wad rise,
  To gie her the long girdin' o't.

But Duncan took her to his wife,
  Ha, ha, the girdin' o't,
To be the comfort o' his life,
  Ha, ha, the girdin' o't.
An' now she scauls baith night an' day
Except when Duncan's at the play –
An' that's as seldom as he may,
  He's weary o' the girdin' o't.

ROBERT BURNS

Carte Postale

Dear Mum and Dad.
                          The picture shows a 'gendarme'
which means policeman. France is overrated.
For two weeks it has been wet. 9th September:
We had a 'degustation' in the Côte
de Maçonnais and Mal got quite light-headed.
Sometimes I think it will be *too* ideal
living with Mal – it's certainly the Real
Thing. I must go now – here comes Mal.
                                      Love, Crystal.

Encircling her slim waist with a fond arm,
the husband of a fortnight nibbles her throat,
would be dismayed to know how she had hated
that first night when in Calais he had kissed all
over her, and oh God!, how she now dreaded
each night the importunate mauve-capped swollen member.

PETER READING

from The Tretis of the Twa Mariit Wemen and the Wedow

Husbands

I

I have ane wallidrag, ane worm, ane auld wobat carl,
A waistit wolroun, na worth but wordis to clatter,
Ane bumbart, ane drone bee, ane bag full of flewme,
Ane scabbit skarth, ane scorpion, ane scutard behind;
To see him scart his awin skin, great scunner I think.
When kissis me that carybald, then kindillis all my sorrow;
As birs of ane brim bear, his beard is als stiff,
But soft and soupill as the silk is his sary lume;
He may well to the sin assent, but saikless is his deidis.
With goreis his twa grim een are gladderit all about,
And gorgeit like twa gutteris that were with glar stoppit;
But when that glowrand ghaist grippis me about,
Then think I hiddowus Mahoun has me in armes;
There may be na sanyne me save fra that auld Satan;
For, though I cross me all clean, fra the crown doun,
He will my corse all beclip, and clap me to his breist.

wallidrag sloven
wobat carl caterpillar
waistit wolroun wild boar
bumbart drone
flewme phlegm
scabbit skarth cormorant
scutard behind shitter
scart scratch
scunner disgust
carybald monster
birs bristles
brim fierce
sary lume sorry tool
saikless innocent
goreis filth
glar mud
sanyne blessing

When schaven is that auld schalk with a scharp rasour,
He schowis on me his schevill mouth, and schedis my lippis;
And with his hard hurcheon skin sa heklis he my cheekis
That as a glemand gleyd glowis my chaftis;
I schrink for the scharp stound, but schout I dare not,
For schore of that auld schrew, schame him betide!
The luve blinkis of that bogill, fra his bleared een,
As Beelzebub had on me blinkt, abasit my spreit . . .
   Ay when that carybold carl wald climb on my wamb,
Then am I dangerous and daine and dour of my will;
Yet let I never that larbar my leggis ga between,
To file my flesh, na fumbill me, without a fee great;
And though his pin puirly me payis in bed,
His purse pays richly in recompense after:
For, or he climb on my corse, that carybald forlane
I have condition of a kerchief of kirsp all there finest,
A gown of engraynit claith, right gaily furrit,
A ring with a royall stane, or other riche jewell,
Or rest of his rusty raid, though he were rede wod . . .
And thus I sell him solace, though I it sour think:
Fra sic a sire, God you save, my sweet sisters dear.

II

My husband was a whure maister, the hugeast in erd,
Therefore I hate him with my heart, sa help me our Lord!

schevill crooked
hurcheon hedgehog
gleyd ember
chaftis jaws
stound pain
schore threatening
daine haughty
larbar impotent man
carybald forlane worthless monster
kirsp all there finest fine fabric
engraynit scarlet
Or rest of his rusty raid foray with a rusty weapon
rede wod stark staring mad

[158]

He is a young man right yaip, but not in youth flouris;
For he is fadit full far and feeblit of strength;
He was as flourishing fresh within this few yearis,
But he is failyeid full far and fulyeid in labour;
He has been lechour so lang while lost is his nature,
His lume is waxit larbar, and lyis in to swoune: . . .
He has been waistit upon wemen, or he me wife chesit,
And in adultery, in my time, I have him tane oft:
And yet he is brankand with bonnet one side,
And blinkand to the brichtest that in the burgh dwellis,
Alse courtly of his clothing and combing of his hair,
As he that is mair valiant in Venus chalmer;
He semis to be something worth, that syphir in bower,
He lukis as he wald luvit be, though he be litill of valour;
He does as dotard dog that damis on all bushis,
And liftis his leg upon loft, though he not list pische;
He has a luke without lust and life without courage;
He has a form without force and fessoun but vertu,
And fair wordis but effect, all fruster of dedis;
He is for ladyis in luve a right lusty schadow,
But in to derne, at the deid, he shall be droop foundin;
He railis and makis repeat with riatus wordis,
Aye rusing him of his raidis and raging in chalmer;
But God wit what I think when he so thra spekis,
And how it settis him so syde to say of sic matteris.

WILLIAM DUNBAR

yaip nimble
failyeid worn out
into swoune in a fainting fit
brankand proud
chalmer chamber
syphir zero
damis pisses
fessoun but vertu show without performance
in to derne in the dark
rusing him of his raidis boasting of his exploits
thra spekis speaks violently
so syde so proudly

And Now You're Ready

And now you're ready who while she was here
Hung like a flag in a calm. Friend, though you stand
Erect and eager, in your eye a tear,
I will not pity you, or lend a hand.

SKYTHINOS
translated by J. V. Cunningham

Rape

canny bord ower there
sharrap man yi think i nowt but tarts

divin na though
wouden mind a bash arrit

hoo pet can a tek yi yem?
am a big strong lad
al luk after yi

a na ya not owld inuff ti suck a dummy

hoo lads tommys scored
whats ya name pet
howear gis a kiss
gis a bit feel pet
di yi fancy a meat injectin?
well jump on the end i this

suck me plums
gis a suck off

o yi commin fora walk wis?
will gan ower the quarry
a nas a shortcut

leave is alen

sharrap or al belt yi

grab a
gis a bit feel
pull a doon
lets have a bit tit
howear man am forst

am warnin yis al git the coppas

sharrap or al kick ya teeth in

pull a doon
rip a skort off
hurry up an stuff it tom
its me next

are man quick
stick it in the get
howld a doon
shi winnit keep still
well hit the twat
please keep still pet an a winnit be a minit
go on man go on
a-a-r-r-r thatsnice

howear well
its me next

TOM PICKARD

Against Coupling

I write in praise of the solitary act:
of not feeling a trespassing tongue
forced into one's mouth, one's breath
smothered, nipples crushed against the
ribcage, and that metallic tingling
in the chin set off by a certain odd nerve:

unpleasure. Just to avoid those eyes would help —
such eyes as a young girl draws life from,
listening to the vegetal
rustle within her, as his gaze
stirs polypal fronds in the obscure
sea-bed of her body, and her own eyes blur.

There is much to be said for abandoning
this no longer novel exercise —
for not 'participating in
a total experience' — when
one feels like the lady in Leeds who
had seen *The Sound of Music* eighty-six times;

or more, perhaps, like the school drama mistress
producing *A Midsummer Night's Dream*
for the seventh year running with
yet another cast from 5B.
Pyramus and Thisbe are dead, but
the hole in the wall can still be troublesome.

I advise you, then, to embrace it without
encumbrance. No need to set the scene,
dress up (or undress), make speeches.
Five minutes of solitude are
enough — in the bath, or to fill
that gap between the Sunday papers and lunch.

FLEUR ADCOCK

IMAGINE

The Young Fellow of King's

There was a young fellow of King's
Who cared not for whores and such things
    For his secret desire
    Was a boy in the choir
With a bum like a jelly on springs.

ANON.

Man and Superman

First he get on the cloak I made him
And he use his X-ray vision on me and say
What colour knickers I got on (though he know anyway).

Then he fly down from what he call the North Pole
(Which is a cupboard) and he save me
From the badness of that Rex bloke.

But he don't see that I'm still under the evil
So I get him with that Krypton stuff
(Which is a paper weighting thing with green bits)

And he go all sapped on the carpet
And he fall for my charms and go mad in love.
But then he use his sheet of lead (which he made of wood),

Which block out the Krypton and he come at me
With all his powers and use his breath
Until he has me under his mercy.

Then he go up and away to his planet
(Which is near the bathroom) and he sleep knowing
That all human people is safe from badness.

CAMERON SELF

Adelaide's Dream

he came in she said he had come in
his mouth was over my nipple here
quietly behind me after we had driven
and I felt it to the bones all the way
in his truck beside him then down
my side a spring pleasure vague except
for his smile he was welling in my
stomach and he touched me black it was
beautiful then we were on between my
legs gently as his mouth the bed and
still it was vague taking down my body
and his body turned so my clothes off
and as he stripped his that before me
I saw his dark legs blackness shone
and you were here and I stroked them
with both hands as well sitting on
that chair but we lay and kissed them
and my mouth was open worried what you
would say for a moment over his phallus
he was holding my buttocks with both
hands his head was between my legs and
his tongue was working along my sex
which wanted inside of my legs and then
into me I wanted all of him to come in
as well touched his phallus with my
tongue first as this tongue working far
in and the tip with its small hole pink
flesh running my skin was off I mean it
was all from the top and down then the
veins my mouth moved up and down then
they stood out on it his shining phallus
sucking playing silk tendrils very warm
it was so hard heavy with little bites
his tongue was my mouth closed on the

top and I let it in me burning I began
to cry go into my mouth deep feeling
that cord with the pleasure of it with
my tongue against the insides of my legs
was the press of his head and then you
were standing naked near the skin of his
face he had turned now his cool black
body I wanted it all I knew that he was
over me and he sucked my breasts near
to coming as the head rosy mouth as he
lay on me now I felt his whole phallus
going in moist in spasms the bed he looked
up he was in me and his thrusts faster
enter me to the core I gripped and you
were over me his sides with my legs
bringing my knees pulsing in my mouth
as my tongue right up with you now
leaning into me then played with it
and I was and you and your phallus
coming too it was all at once was in
my mouth too I felt the warm stiff as
he came into me the huge hardness of it
there and sucked it and my hands warm
spurts rocking me held your legs
pressing so that I moaned and as I came
down over him you into me like spring
rains and your seeds spurted into my
mouth and we were all moving at once
in white jets I swallowed moaning I do
not know how long we lay there
afterwards I believe
we began again
with the Chinese girl
who must have come through the window
up to her thigh as she straddled
the sill I saw the black arm reach out

and hand take her down and was
running his hand under the knee
the dress pulled around her bottom
turned her over and I could not resist
giving a little suck pulled her dress
off her very black and as he held her
breasts from behind hair thrown out
across your phallus his black thighs
closed in on the rounds now so near
my mouth again of her buttocks and I
saw the whole length and I stood up
over her back offering his phallus slowly
drive into her she my sex to his mouth
his tongue was rocking back and forth
on him gently in me against my legs
holding his head under me I felt softness
her skin she had moved her head the
Chinese girl rocking and moaning sweetly
against the backs of my legs to take you
into her mouth then we changed places
you were in me between the Chinese girl's
thighs her warm and hard and he was over
me until I don't know how you were in
her his phallus in my mouth his head
so you could hold her knees and me
under him as I saw your mouth close
on her little left breast and his close
on the monkey came in the monkey came
in her right breast and planted on our
happy moaning mound and beat his chest
jumping his hairy feet and screaming
he was very hairy

CHRISTOPHER MIDDLETON

Would I were Changed

Jove, for Europa's love, took shape of bull,
And, for Callisto, played Diana's part,
And, in a golden shower, he filled full
The lap of Danaë with celestial art.
Would I were changed but to my mistress' gloves,
That those white lovely fingers I might hide,
That I might kiss those hands, which mine heart loves,
Or else, that chain of pearl, her neck's vain pride,
Made proud with her neck's veins, that I might fold
About that lovely neck, and her paps tickle,
Or her to compass, like a belt of gold,
Or that sweet wine, which down her throat doth trickle,
To kiss her lips, and lie next to her heart,
Run through her veins, and pass by pleasure's part.

BARNABE BARNES

A Very Shocking Poem Found among the Papers of an Eminent Victorian Divine

I saw you with Septimus on the parterre
    In front of the Old Bishop's Palace.
The sunshine was weaving its gold in your hair
    But my heart was embittered and malice
Moved in me mightily; jealous was I
    And I burned with desire to distress you,
To down-thunder like Jove from that clear summer sky
    And at once, then and there, to undress you!

That hand, once in mine, was in his as you walked
    And answered him in your bright treble;
Not a word could I hear but I knew that you talked
    And the Flesh rose up like a dark rebel –
For that hand, as I knew, was an adjunct to Love,
    Like a hot caper sauce to hot mutton,
And designed by the Lord to descend from above
    First to fondle – and then to unbutton!

Ah! those feet that ran to me won't run to me now,
    The dismal and desperate fact is
They will turn to avoid me, for you will know how
    To go home with the Choir after Practice –
Though you lingered once sweetly to dally with me
    And our preoccupations weren't choral
As you sat in the sitting-room there on my knee
    And the examination was oral!

I saw those eyes opening, gazing at him
 With the blue of the midsummer heaven,
My own eyes with traitorous tear-drops grew dim
 And of Rage, lustful Rage, a black leaven
Worked in me there; for those eyes once had seen
 (Thought to break my heart, break it and rive it)
On the ottoman, proud in its velvety green,
 Those parts that our God has called private!

I dream of a Paradise still, now and then,
 But it is not the orthodox milieu
Where good spirits abound – with no women or men.
 Ah! My Conscience lies drowned like Ophelia!
And my Heaven's a dream of an opulent South
 With soft cushions, wine, perfumes, bells ringing,
My member for ever held tight in your mouth
 And a thousand bright choirboys all singing!

GAVIN EWART

4th Song *from 77 Dream Songs*

Filling her compact & delicious body
with chicken páprika, she glanced at me
twice.
Fainting with interest, I hungered back
and only the fact of her husband & four other people
kept me from springing on her

or falling at her little feet and crying
'You are the hottest one for years of night
Henry's dazed eyes
have enjoyed, Brilliance.' I advanced upon
(despairing) my spumoni. – Sir Bones: is stuffed,
de world, wif feeding girls.

– Black hair, complexion Latin, jewelled eyes
downcast . . . The slob beside her   feasts . . . What wonders is
she sitting on, over there?
The restaurant buzzes. She might as well be on Mars.
Where did it all go wrong? There ought to be a law against
    Henry.
– Mr Bones: there is.

JOHN BERRYMAN

The Pitman's Lovesong

Aw wish my lover she was a cherry
Growing upon yon cherry tree,
And aw mysel a bonny blackbird;
How aw would peck that cherry cherree.

Aw wish my lover she was a red rose
Growing upon yon garden wa',
And aw mysel was a butterflee;
O on that red rosie aw wad fa'.

Aw wish my lover she was a fish
Sooming doon in the saut sea,
And aw mysel was a fisher lad;
O aw wad catch her reet cunningly.

Aw wish my love was in a kist
And aw mysel to carry the key.
Then aw wad gan tin her when aw had list,
And bear my hinny good company.

Aw wish my love she was a grey ewe
Grazing by yonder river side,
And aw mysel a bonny black tup;
O on that ewie how aw wad ride.

O she's bonny, she wondrous canny,
O she's well far'd to see,
For the mair aw think on my love's on upon her,
And under her apron fain wad aw be.

Aw wish my lover she was a bee skep,
And aw mysel a bumble bee,
That aw might be a lodger within her;
She's sweeter than honey or honeycombe tea.

Aw wish my lover was a ripe turd,
Smoking doon in yon dyke side,
And aw mysel was a shitten flee;
Aw'd sook her all up before she was dried.

O my hinny, my bonny hinny,
O my hinny, my bonny hinnee;
The mair aw think on her, my heart's set upon her.
She's fairer than ever she used to be.

ANON.

Toilet

I wonder will I speak to the girl
sitting opposite me on this train.
I wonder will my mouth open and say,
'Are you going all the way
to Newcastle?' or 'Can I get you a coffee?'
Or will it simply go 'aaaaah'
as if it had a mind of its own?

Half closing eggshell blue eyes,
she runs her hand through her hair
so that it clings to the carriage cloth;
then slowly frees itself.
She finds a brush and her long fair hair
flies back and forth like an African fly-whisk,
making me feel dizzy.

Suddenly, without warning,
she packs it all away in a rubber band
because I have forgotten to look out
the window for a moment.
A coffee is granted permission
to pass between her lips
and does so eagerly, without fuss.

A tunnel finds us looking out the window
into one another's eyes. She leaves her seat,
but I know that she likes me
because the light saying 'TOILET'
has come on, a sign that she is lifting
her skirt, taking down her pants
and peeing all over my face.

HUGO WILLIAMS

A Plea for Mercy

For all the poor little sods who shoot themselves off
in boarding schools and dormitories, jerking into sleep,

and all the prissy girls who ride their horses bareback
or wet their knickers and seats at noisy pop concerts,

there are always the others who will, in the end, read
Divinity, or spend the rest of their life praying

to that pregnant girl, or join the prison service,
clamping an eye to the hole in the locked cell door.

In mental hospitals the patients masturbate quite openly,
with dreamy spiritual faraway faces, not much to lose,

and knowing they are listed for the high jump next day
anyway, passing the uneven hours between doctor's rounds

and basket making. If they go blind, they should care.
In the penumbra of their distorted world so many shadows,

and such fragile transparent pleasures. From dormitories
to geriatric homes and all the institutions in between,

a fair fantasy, a brief respite, and a dreamless sleep,
before the matrons, doctors, screws and curates muscle in.

ELIZABETH BARTLETT

The Vine

I dreamed this mortal part of mine
Was metamorphosed to a vine;
Which crawling one and every way,
Enthralled my dainty Lucia.
Me thought, her long small legs and thighs
I with my tendrils did surprise;
Her belly, buttocks, and her waist
By now soft nervelets were embraced:
About her head I writhing hung,
And with rich clusters (hid among
The leaves) her temples I behung
So that my Lucia seemed to me
Young Bacchus ravished by his tree.
My curls about her neck did crawl,
And arms and hands they did enthral:
So that she could not freely stir,
(All parts there made one prisoner).
But when I crept with leaves to hide
Those parts, which maids keep unespied,
Such fleeting pleasures there I took,
That with the fancy I awoke;
And found (Ah me!) this flesh of mine
More like a stock, than like a vine.

ROBERT HERRICK

she being Brand

she being Brand

-new; and you
know consequently a
little stiff i was
careful of her and (having

thoroughly oiled the universal
joint tested my gas felt of
her radiator made sure her springs were O.

K.) i went right to it flooded-the-carburetor cranked her

up, slipped the
clutch (and then somehow got into reverse she
kicked what
the hell) next
minute i was back in neutral tried and

again slo-wly; bare,ly nudg. ing (my

lev-er Right-
oh and her gears being in
A 1 shape passed
from low through
second-in-to-high like
greasedlightning) just as we turned the corner of Divinity

avenue i touched the accelerator and give

her the juice, good

                    (it
was the first ride and believe i we was
happy to see how nice she acted right up to
the last minute coming back down by the Public
Gardens i slammed on
the

internalexpanding
&
externalcontracting
brakes Bothatonce and

brought allof her tremB
-ling
to a:dead.

stand-
;Still)

                    e e cummings

The Hammam Name

From a poem by a Turkish Lady

Winsome Torment rose from slumber, rubbed his eyes, and
   went his way
Down the street towards the Hammam. Goodness gracious!
   people say,
What a handsome countenance! The Sun has risen twice to-
   day!
And as for the Undressing Room it quivered in dismay.
With the glory of his presence see the window panes
   perspire,
And the water in the basin boils and bubbles with desire.

Now his lovely cap is treated like a lover; off it goes!
Next his belt the boy unbuckles; down it falls, and at his
   toes
All the growing heap of garments buds and blossoms like a
   rose.
Last of all his shirt came flying. Ah, I tremble to disclose
How the shell came off the almond, how the lily showed its
   face,
How I saw a silver mirror taken flashing from its case.

He was gazed upon so hotly that his body grew too hot,
So the bathman seized the adorers and expelled them on the
   spot;
Then the desperate shampooer his propriety forgot,
Stumbled when he brought the pattens, fumbled when he
   tied a knot,
And remarked when musky towels had obscured his idol's
   hips,
See Love's Plenilune, Mashallah, in a partial eclipse!

Desperate the loofah wriggled: soap was melted instantly:
All the bubble hearts were broken. Yes, for them as well as
    me,
Bitterness was born of beauty; as for the shampooer, he
Fainted, till a jug of water set the Captive Reason free.
Happy bath! The baths of heaven cannot wash their spotted
    moon:
You are doing well with this one. Not a spot upon him
    soon!

Now he leaves the luckless bath for fear of setting it alight;
Seizes on a yellow towel growing yellower in fright,
Polishes the pearly surface till it burns disastrous bright,
And a bathroom window shatters in amazement at the
    sight.
Like the fancies of a dreamer frail and soft his garments
    shine
As he robes a mirror body shapely as a poet's line.

Now upon his cup of coffee see the lips of Beauty bent:
And they perfume him with incense and they sprinkle him
    with scent,
Cal him Bey and call him Pasha, and receive with deep
    content
The gratuities he gives them, smiling and indifferent.
Out he goes: the mirror strains to kiss her darling; out he
    goes!
Since the flame is out, the water can but freeze.
                                        The water froze.

                                JAMES ELROY FLECKER

Nude

The door is open and yes she is naked,
The blonde at the basin cleaning her teeth.
I and her toothbrush are over-excited;
I could catch her quivering rump and eat it
Now as she steps through the steam to the bath.

Her skin wears a two-piece of next to no suntan.
And striped in brown and orange (just like mine)
A flannel, saving energy for later,
Floats in the warm promiscuous water.
Soap and flannel are lucky men.

Sweat on the mirror. Soap in its slime.
Waters have issued, the plughole has moaned
And the bath is empty except for the scum,
The dead hairs, puddle and dirty rim.
She was on two counts not a real blonde.

DUNCAN FORBES

Personal Advertisement

TASTY GEEZER/STUCK IN SNEEZER/YEAR BEFORE/GETS
   OUT/
SEEKS/SLOW-WITTED/GIANT-TITTED/SOCIOLOGIST
   VISITOR/
WHO LIKES/TO MESS ABOUT/

BLOKE NEEDS POKE/SEND PICS/BOX 6/

MASON/COUNCILLOR/MAGISTRATE/SOMETIME/
CONSERVATIVE/CANDIDATE/JOGGER/SQUASH-PLAYER/
   FIRST-CLASS SHAPE/
SEEKS SIMILAR/VIEW RAPE/

BLOKE NEEDS POKE/SEND PICS/BOX 6/

SAD DOG/SEEKS TAIL/OLD BEAST/GROWN FRAIL/
   SNIFFING/
WORLD/FEELS MORE THAN/BITOUTOF/HELL WITH THAT/
   HUNTS/
OLDER CAT/TO MEET/GRAB/BEAT THE/SHITOUTOF/

BLOKE NEEDS POKE/SEND PICS/BOX 6/

WHAT/THE WINTER/NEEDS/IS STARLIGHT/WHAT/THE
   BLIND MAN/
NEEDS/IS LUCK/WHAT DIS BOY/NEED IS A/WEEK IN DE/
   SACK/
WID WUNNADEM/REAL/BIGASS SISTERS/DAT/COMES/LIKE
   A TRUCK/

BLOKE NEEDS POKE/SEND PICS/BOX 6/

LONG-FACED/LANKY/EVANGELICAL/WIFE EVANGELICAL/
  INTEREST/
SANKEY/MOTHER-IN-LAW/EVANGELICAL/CRANKY/SEEKS
  ANYBODY/
VIEW/HANKY-PANKY/

BLOKE NEEDS POKE/SEND PICS/BOX 6/

PRIME MINISTER/FANCYING/CHANGE OF PACE/PLANS
  SPOT OF/
NONSENSE/BACK AT HER PLACE/ON REGULAR BASIS/NO
  AIRS/
GRACES/WOMEN OR MEN/POP IN/FOR A NAUGHTY/AT NO
  TEN/

ONE PART/IRISH/THREE PARTS/PISSED/SIX FOOT/SEVEN
  AND/
NEVER BEEN/KISSED/WHERE/ARE YOU/

BLOKE NEEDS POKE/BOX 6/
FORGET ABOUT THE PICS
       KIT WRIGHT

On the Low Status of Masturbation

Old arguments that it's injurious
Are known today to be quite spurious:
It's intelligent if kids are curious.

But it's something that we don't discuss
In conversation on the bus.
Besides, it's others more than us.

For screwing's always fit to spout
And VD you can moan about,
But wanking hasn't any clout.

CHARLES THOMSON

from The Alchemist

MAMMON
I will have all my beds blown up, not stuffed:
Down is too hard; and then mine oval room
Filled with such pictures as Tiberius took
From Elephantis, and dull Aretine
But coldly imitated. Then, my glasses
Cut in more subtle angles, to disperse
And multiply the figures, as I walk
Naked between my *succubae*. My mists
I'll have of perfume, vapoured 'bout the room,
To lose our selves in; and my baths, like pits
To fall into, from whence we will come forth,
And roll us dry in gossamer and roses . . .
            . . . Where I spy
A wealthy citizen, or rich lawyer,
Have a sublimed, pure wife, unto that fellow
I'll send a thousand pounds to be my cuckold.

FACE
And I shall carry it?

MAMMON
                  No, I'll ha' no bawds
But fathers and mothers – they will do it best,
Best of all others. And my flatterers
Shall be the pure and gravest of divines
That I can get for money. My mere fools
Eloquent burgesses, and then my poets
The same that writ so subtly of the fart,
Whom I will entertain still for that subject.
The few that would give out themselves to be
Court- and town- stallions and each-where bely
Ladies who are known most innocent, for them,
These will I beg to make me eunuchs of,
And they shall fan me with ten estrich tails

Apiece, made in a plume to gather wind.
We will be brave, Puff, now we ha' the med'cine.
My meat shall all come in, in Indian shells,
Dishes of agate set in gold; and studded
With emeralds, sapphires, hyacinths, and rubies.
The tongues of carps, dormice, and camels' heels,
Boiled i' the spirit of Sol, and dissolved pearl
(Apicius' diet 'gainst the epilepsy);
And I will eat these broths with spoons of amber,
Headed with diamond and carbuncle.
My foot-boy shall eat pheasants, calvered salmons,
Knots, godwits, lampreys. I myself will have
The beards of barbels served instead of salads;
Oiled mushrooms, and the swelling, unctuous paps
Of a fat pregnant sow, newly cut off,
Dressed with an exquisite and poignant sauce;
For which, I'll say unto my cook, 'There's gold;
Go forth and be a knight!'

BEN JONSON

Ways of Skinning a Cat

A butch body-builder from Brum
Was wholly unable to come
    Till he tried masturbation
    In rapt contemplation
Of pics of his muscular bum.

MIKE THURLOW

Soho

dutch straps mr universe jock caps 1001 nights genuine
   rechy
fully tested adolescence & box 5/- only velazquez
kalpa baggers naturist bargain guide original sex carpet
sutra hill transvestism before marriage more inside
kama books fanny goods family nudes free each purch
planning our own petronius durex opedia
history of the genet established insertion imported
lubricated health best of the flowers
human hygienic capital rod no obligatio
lash purgated quatrefoil masochism
unex punishment trusses george ryley scott soft yet firm
5 capital practices for men 7/6 ea
life of skin thin witchcraft variants
technique of hirschf strap psycho many lands nus
homosex encyclo erotica the set nothing like the sun
30/- psycholo oriental rubber burton leather boys
author of amazing years of diaphragm
desire and pursuit of the marquis de sutra au cinéma
health & wrestling jours de sodom unbeatable
william burroughs shakespeare complete dead fingers
cacti and succulent flagellation havelock and after
handy pathia sexu ellis ready reckoner
rhythm method works quentin per crisp cent
ten tom jones tablets belt recommended
our lady of the litesome
wuthering heights full protection
boxing & vaseline fully illustrated hosiery
ABZ of unrepeatable tropic of enemas
who's afraid of virginia goldfinger
dr no guide to london heller orgies book of the f
20,000 leagues under angus wilson yoga fetishism agency
traps omar khayyam a week's supply for pocket torture
   photogr

chinese medical cooking in 80 days lo duca come in and
   browse
trial of oscar mickey fleming birth-cont catch-22 hyde miller
no mean city of night prophylactic burgess anomalies
johnson & johnson john o'hara john calder judo spillane
   karate
transparent KY water soluble cookbook
an unhurried view of impotence rock plants and alpines
oxford book of english prostitution
youth requisites sterilized plain white
slightly washable shop soiled down the ages
But to wash London
               would take a sea.
To want to wash it
            history.

Now bury this poem in one of the vaults
of our civilization, and let the Venusian
computers come down, and searching for life
   crack our ghastly code.
Bury it, bury it! Who cares?
   We shall never know.
We've buried worse, with mouths to feed.
   And so . . . And so . . . And so . . .
Polish the window, bury the poem, and go.

EDWIN MORGAN

Underneath the Archers *or*
What's All This about Walter's Willy?

Everyone's on about Walter's willy
   Down at the Bull tonight.
He'd done Dan's sheep and he's done them silly –
He's had young Phil and his daughter's filly –
   And folk don't think it's right.

   Folk *know* it can't be right.

No, the chat's not prim and the chat's not proper,
   Down at the Bull tonight,
'Cos everyone's on about Walter's whopper
And telling tales of his terrible chopper –
   And folk don't think it's right.

Sid Perks has drained the bitter cup
   Down at the Bull tonight.
Can't stand . . . or sit . . . or speak . . . or sup . . .
Walter got him while bottling up –
   And folk don't think it's right.

   Folk *know* it can't be right.

He got poor Polly while drawing a cork
   Down at the Bull tonight.
And Doris is still too ill to talk –
And Mrs Perkins can hardly *walk* –
   And folk don't think it's right.

There's in-depth discussion of every facet,
   Down at the Bull tonight,
Of Walter's gigantic natural asset –
Carries as far as Penny Hasset –
   (Folk know *that* can't be right)

   Folk *know* it can't be right.

Poor old Dan's a broken man
    Down at the Bull tonight.
Got locked in the back of Walter's van
With its ghastly height, unearthly span –
    And folk don't think it's right.

Found him alone in the woods on Sunday
    (Down at the Bull tonight),
Had him all day and most of Monday –
That was the end of poor Joe Grundy –
    Folk don't think it's right.

    Folk *know* it can't be right.

It wasn't a Gainsborough nor an El Greco
    (Down at the Bull tonight)
Brought dozens of coach-loads out for a dekko –
But a photo-fit in the *Borchester Echo* –
    Folk don't think it's right.

Nobody understands it fully,
    Down at the Bull tonight,
The monstrous range of it. Was it by pulley
It scaled Grey Gables and whopped Jack Woolley?
    Folk don't think it's right.

    Folk *know* it can't be right.

There's coaches come from Ware and Wigan,
    Down at the Bull tonight,
From Wales and Wallasey, out for a swig an'
A sizing-up of Walter's big 'un –
    And folk don't think it's right.

Yes, everyone's on about Walter's thuggery,
    Down at the Bull tonight,
His *cattle*-courting, his *sheep* skullduggery,
Piggery jiggery-pokery buggery –
    Folk don't think it's right.

Folk *know* it can't be right.

Even the Vicar's been muttering, 'F— it,'
  Down at the Bull tonight,
'There's nowhere left he hasn't stuck it –
I *wish* old Walter would kick the bucket –
  He knows it can't be right!'

Folk know it CAN'T BE RIGHT!

KIT WRIGHT

Making Love to Marilyn Monroe

He pumps her up, po-faced, his right leg rising
And falling wearisomely. Breasts inflate,
Thighs fatten, force and perseverance raising
A rubber spectre. Plump, comical feet
Swell into being, but her eyes stay dead.
Her crotch arrives; exaggerated, furry.

Five minutes and she's full. Pink. Somewhat odd.
His brother brought her over on the ferry
From Hook of Holland, folded flat beneath
Shirts and trousers. Bought in Amsterdam,
She needed only an awakening breath,
Divine afflatus nurturing the dream

Till it becomes substantial. When she's tight
He plugs her with a stopper, tests for leaks
With an embrace, marvels at each huge teat,
And stands back slightly to admire her looks.
She leans against the sofa at an angle,
Legs amply parted, lips a sullen pout.

Like Mae West she might mutter, 'I'm no angel'
If able to articulate. Her pert
Expression is the only clue he'll get
To how she feels. If he but had a wand
He'd *ping* her into life, but all she's got
To offer him is quick relief and wind.

He gets it over with, lights turned down low.
Pneumatic gasps were absent. Self-esteem
Plummets, yet she was an easy lay.
He puts her in the wardrobe till next time.
The sorry fact is real women don't
Fancy him. A shrink would understand.

Who are so inflated that no dent
Disfigures them? Some men need to get stoned
Before they do it; some touch little girls . . .
At least this shady rigmarole can bring
Release without distress. Contentment gels.
Doubt punctures with a quintessential bang.

PAUL GROVES

WICKED WORDS

The Young Fellow of Wadham

There was a young fellow of Wadham
Who asked for a ticket to Sodom.
      When they said, 'We prefer
      Not to issue them, sir,'
He said, 'Don't call me Sir, call me Modom!'

                ANON.

Rite of Spring

So winter closed its fist
And got it stuck in the pump.
The plunger froze up a lump

In its throat, ice founding itself
Upon iron. The handle
Paralysed at an angle.

Then the twisting of wheat straw
Into ropes, lapping them tight
Round stem and snout, then a light

That sent the pump up in flame.
It cooled, we lifted her latch,
Her entrance was wet, and she came.

SEAMUS HEANEY

The Semantic Limerick According to the Shorter Oxford English Dictionary (1933)

There existed an adult male person who had lived a relatively short time, belonging or pertaining to St John's,* who desired to commit sodomy with the large web-footed swimming birds of the genus *Cygnus* or subfamily *Cygninae* of the family *Anatidae*, characterized by a long and gracefully curved neck and a majestic motion when swimming.

So he moved into the presence of the person employed to carry burdens, who declared: 'Hold or possess as something at your disposal my female child! The large web-footed swimming-birds of the genus *Cygnus* or subfamily *Cygninae* of the family *Anatidae*, characterized by a long and gracefully curved neck and a majestic motion when swimming, are set apart, specially retained for the Head, Fellows and Tutors of the College!'

* *A College of Cambridge University.*

The Semantic Limerick According to Dr Johnson's Dictionary (Edition of 1765)

There exifted a person, not a woman or a boy, being in the firft part of life, not old, of St John's,* who wifhed to — the large water-fowl, that have a long and very ftraight neck, and are very white, excepting when they are young (their legs and feet being black, as are their bills, which are like that of a goofe, but fomething rounder, and a little hooked at the lower ends, the two fides below their eyes being black and fhining like ebony).

In confequence of this he moved ftep by ftep to the one that had charge of the gate, who pronounced: 'Poffefs and enjoy my female offspring! The large water-fowl, that have a long and very ftraight neck, and are very white, excepting when they are young (their legs and feet being black, as are their bills, which are like that of a goofe, but fomething rounder, and a little hooked at the lower ends, the two fides below their eyes being black and fhining like ebony), are kept in ftore, laid up for a future time, for the fake of the gentlemen with Spanish titles.'

* *A College of Cambridge University.*

GAVIN EWART

Verse for a Birthday Card

Many happy returns and good luck
When it comes to a present, I'm stuck.
>   If you weren't far away
>   On your own special day,
I could give you a really nice glass of lager.

WENDY COPE

Song

Does the policeman sleep with his boots on,
                        with his helmet on,
                        with his boots on?
Does the policeman sleep with his boots on
with his whistle at the ready on his pad?

GERDA MAYER

Discuss the Influence of Posture upon Bodily Function. Give up to Twelve Examples.

(University of Manchester Final B.Sc. Honours Paper in Physiology)

It's hard to spit far when you're doing the limbo
to make love to a horse if your arms are akimbo

to defecate cleanly while stood on your head
to chew your left buttock if lying in bed.

If you glide under water it's tricky to sneeze.
It's hard to lick earlobes when down on your knees.

When you stand on one leg it's not easy to piss.
If you hang by the neck it's less simple to kiss.

You can't hop with your knees in a sideways direction.
If you sit on your balls you may gain an erection.

You can't walk a tightrope while doing the splits.
If you lie on your stomach you can't swing your tits.

JOHN LATHAM

Sea Poem

I must go down to the sea again
For a sail and a tot of rum,
A 'Hello Sailor', a futtock's end
And the warmth of a cabin boy's smile.

JOHN ROBINSON

Spelling It Out

Jain dusent ware enny.
What credence could we give
to such a two-a-penny

scrawl? And who wrote it?
It looked like the hand
that chalked, *I suked Jens tits.*

Did someone have inside knowledge?
And did this learning
take place under the bridge

where we ogled
such titbits of urban pornography?
The orthography

left much to be desired,
the content even more.
But what most fired

us was neither former nor latter
but last in this illiterate triad:
I dun Jan wit a frennsh leter.

ROBERT MAITRE

A Special Theory of Relativity

According to Einstein
There's no still centre of the universe:
Everything is moving
Relative to something else.
My love, I move myself towards you,
Measure my motion
In relation to yours.

According to Einstein
The mass of a moving body
Exceeds its mass
When standing still.
My love, in moving
Through you
I feel my mass increase.

According to Einstein
The length of a moving body
Diminishes
As speed increases.
My love, after accelerating
Inside you
I spectacularly shrink.

According to Einstein
Time slows down
As we approach
The speed of light.
My love, as we approach
The speed of light
Time is standing still.

ALAN BOLD

Victorian Guitar
for David Hammond

*Inscribed 'Belonged to Louisa Catherine Coe before
her marriage to John Charles Smith, March 1852.'*

I expected the lettering to carry
The date of the gift, a kind of christening:
This is more like the plate on a coffin.

Louisa Catherine Smith could not be light.
Far more than a maiden name
Was cancelled by him on the first night.

I believe he cannot have known your touch
Like this instrument – for clearly
John Charles did not hold with fingering –

Which is obviously a lady's:
The sound-box trim as a girl in stays,
The neck right for the smallest span.

Did you even keep track of it as a wife?
Do you know the man who has it now
Is giving it the time of its life?

SEAMUS HEANEY

Viola d'Amore

'Woman is a delightful instrument, of which love is the bow, and man the artist.' Stendhal

She was his instrument, and oh,
How well he wielded love's bow.
At any hour, in any key,
He played with virtuosity.

But after years of harmony
She started losing her *esprit*,
And then her bridge began to crack . . .
He lost a screw, his bow went slack.
Her F-holes warped, her belly swelled,
She creaked whenever she was held.
His fiddling became erratic,
His technique merely automatic.
Appassionatas soon gave way
To rallentandos, then, no play.

One day he placed her on the shelf,
And humming softly to himself,
Put on his coat and left, hell bent,
To find a better instrument.

JOAN VAN POZNAK

The Love Song of Tommo Frogley

Comeahead then comeahead
When the skies round Birkie turn tomater red
Like some ould heartcase breathalysed in a copshop;
Comeahead past tellies on the blink
An bashed-in bins that stink:
Past playgrounds strewed with soupcans rubbers rocks
An offies gorrup like Fort Knox . . .
O comeahead I dare yer
An see ar NO GO area

In twos an twos the busies comes an goes
Chattin back ter their radios

The fog that hangs around the ferries
Squeezed out a sock near Fort Perch Rock
Squeezed out an udder one near Formby Light
Picked at its athlete's foot by Crosby baths
Towelled itself down against the floating roadway
Coughed up its lungs at Tranmere
Then crashed a lobbo job dead snug-an-tite

An there will be time
Fer me to go meet me peergroup in the dump;
Ter roll a drunk or give some cow a hump
An time ter wire another horseless carriage
Or have a gangshag in a broke-in garage
Time ter do what we goan ter do
Before we sit round sniffing bags of glue

In twos an twos the busies comes an goes
Chattin back ter their radios

An there will be time
Ter do Park Road at ninety
(Cornering on one wheel)
Time ter bomb up the wrong cider the street
An make them oul age parasites use their feet

Puttin me foot down like I meant it
When all them copcars go demented . . .
An Time fer me Legal Aid ter lodge an appeal

Cos I've knowed the courthouse gobshites knowed them all
Probation prats that set yer 'aims' an 'goals'
I've wrote me name all round with aerosols . . .

An I've knowed the juries cos they're all the same
The ones that seem ter know yer family name . . .

An I've knowed me Risley oppos knowed them all
The scabby ones as smelly as ar dog
(If fights kick off their sleeping like a log)
The snides the no-marks an the maniacs
The ones that's away with the mixer;
The crapheads an the nutters an the mongs
I wooden touch with a tongs . . .

Have yer gorra toke of smack? Lets go roll another quare
I'll slip me crombie on an hang round Falkner Square
An watch them prostitutes that hang round there

(Yer don't get in those jellyboxes free)

I've seed them swigging sherry on a step
Posing in kinky boots an plastic macs
Fer trade in shades an beatup Cadillacs

In bed yer dream yer smashed on highclass grass
With highclass prosties (like yer get from phone ads)
Till scuffer toecaps tap yer in the gonads.

ROGER CRAWFORD

[213]

from Strugnell's Sonnets

The expense of spirits is a crying shame,
So is the cost of wine. What bard today
Can live like old Khayyam? It's not the same –
A loaf and thou and Tesco's Beaujolais.
I had this bird called Sharon, fond of gin –
Could knock back six or seven. At the price
I paid a high wage for each hour of sin
And that was why I only had her twice.
Then there was Tracy, who drank rum and Coke,
So beautiful I didn't mind at first
But love grows colder. Now some other bloke
Is subsidizing Tracy and her thirst.
I need a woman, honest and sincere,
Who'll come across on half a pint of beer.

WENDY COPE

On First Looking into Krafft-Ebing's
   Psychopathosexualis

Much have I travelled in those realms of old
Where many a whore in hall-doors could be seen
Of many a bonnie brothel and shebeen
Which bawds connived at by policemen hold.
I too have listened while the Quay was coaled,
But never did I taste the Pure obscene –
Much less imagine that my past was clean –
Till this Krafft-Ebing out his story told.
Then felt I rather taken by surprise
As on the evening when I met Macran,
And retrospective thoughts and doubts did rise,
Was I quite normal when my life began
With love that leans towards rural sympathies,
Potent behind a cart with Mary Ann?

OLIVER ST JOHN GOGARTY

The Decanonization

For Godsake just stay still and let me come.
Why *do* you keep on going in and out?
There must be something you can think about
To hold off for a bit. At least slow down.
Try conjugating verbs in French,
Compose a Treatise on Defence,
Pretend you're sitting on a Bench,
Prepare a speech or do a sum,
So you will let me come.

SYLVIA KANTARIS

On the Ambivalence of Male Contact Sports

Among men who play Rugger
you seldom find a bugger –
nobody strokes a bum
in the scrum.
Nevertheless . . .

GAVIN EWART

NAME CALLING

Dryden

Dryden in vain tried this nice way of wit,
For he to be a tearing blade thought fit,
But when he would be sharp he still was blunt,
To frisk his frolic fancy he'd cry Cunt,
Would give the ladies a dry, bawdy bob,
And thus he got the name of Poet Squab.

JOHN WILMOT, EARL OF ROCHESTER

Upon the Author of the Play Called *Sodom*

Tell me, abandoned miscreant, prithee tell
What damned power, invoked and sent from Hell
(If Hell were bad enough), did thee inspire
To write what fiends, ashamed, would blushing hear?
Hast thou of late embraced some succubus
And used the lewd familiar for a Muse?
Or didst thy soul by inch o' the candle sell,
To gain the glorious name of pimp to Hell?
If so, go, and its vowed allegiance swear;
Without press-money be its volunteer.
May he who envies thee deserve thy fate,
Deserve both Heaven's and mankind's scorn and hate.
Disgrace to libels! Foil to very shame!
Whom 'tis a scandal to vouchsafe to damn!
What foul description's foul enough for thee,
Sunk quite below the reach of infamy?
Thou covetest to be lewd, but want'st the might,
And art all over devil but in wit.
Weak, feeble strainer at mere ribaldry,
Whose Muse is impotent to that degree
It had need, like age, to be whipped to lechery.

Vile sot! who clapped with poetry art sick,
And void'st corruption like a shankered prick,
Like ulcers, thy impostumed, addle brains
Drop out in matter, which thy paper stains:
Whence nauseous rhymes by filthy births proceed,
As maggots in some turd-engendering breed.
Thy Muse has got the flowers, and they ascend,
As in some greensick girl, at upper end.
Sure Nature made, or meant at least to have done 't,
Thy tongue a clitoris, thy mouth a cunt.

by inch o' the candle sell a timed auction

How well a dildo would that place become,
To gag it up and make it forever dumb!
At least it should be syringed —
Or wear some stinking merkin for a beard,
That all from its base converse might be scared:
As they a door shut up, and mark 't beware,
That tells infection, and the Plague is there.

Though Moorfields author! fit for bawds to quote
(If bawds themselves with honour safe may do 't)
When suburb-prentice comes to hire delight,
And wants incentives to dull appetite,
There punk, perhaps, may thy brave works rehearse,
Frigging the senseless thing with hand and verse;
Which after shall, (preferred to dressing-box)
Hold turpentine and medicines for the pox:
Or (if I may ordain a fate more fit
For such foul, nasty excrements of wit)
May they, condemned, to the public jakes be lent,
(For me, I'd fear the piles of vengeance sent
Should I with them profane my fundament)
There bugger wiping porters when they shite,
And so thy book itself turn sodomite.

JOHN OLDHAM

So Help Me God

So help me God, I couldn't choose between
Smelling Aemilius head-on or behind:
His mouth and arse are equally unclean.
Well no, perhaps the latter's more refined,
Being toothless, for the mouth shows yard-long teeth,
Gums like a worn-out cart-frame with parts missing,
And a grin that stretches like the cunt beneath
An old mule on a hot day when she's pissing.
He fucks the girls and fancies he's got charm.
Why don't we post him to the grinding wheel
To drive the donkeys on a penal farm?
As for a woman who's prepared to feel
Aemilius, she'd fondle a diseased
Hangman and lick him anywhere he pleased.

CATULLUS
translated by James Michie

A Satire on Charles II

I' th' isle of Britain, long since famous grown
For breeding the best cunts in Christendom,
There reigns, and oh! long may he reign and thrive,
The easiest King and best-bred man alive.
Him no ambition moves to get renown
Like the French fool, that wanders up and down
Serving his people, hazarding his crown.
Peace is his aim, his gentleness is such,
And love he loves, for he loves fucking much.
   Nor are his high desires above his strength:
His sceptre and his prick are of a length;
And she may sway the one who plays with th'other,
And make him little wiser than his brother.
Poor prince! thy prick, like thy buffoons at Court,
Will govern thee because it makes thee sport.
'Tis sure the sauciest prick that e'er did swive,
The proudest, peremptoriest prick alive.
Though safety, law, religion, life lay on 't,
'Twould break through all to make its way to cunt.
Restless he rolls about from whore to whore,
A merry monarch, scandalous and poor.
   To Carwell, the most dear of all his dears,
The best relief of his declining years,
Oft he bewails his fortune, and her fate:
To love so well, and be beloved so late.
For though in her he settles well his tarse,
Yet his dull, graceless ballocks hang an arse.
This you'd believe, had I but time to tell ye
The pains it cost to poor, laborious Nelly,

hang an arse be slow

Whilst she employs hands, fingers, lips and thighs
Ere she can raise the member she enjoys.
    All monarchs I hate, and the thrones they sit on,
From the hector of France to the cully of Britain.

JOHN WILMOT, EARL OF ROCHESTER

His Tool was Large

His tool was large and so was his nose,
Papylus could smell it whenever it rose.

MARTIAL
translated by Fiona Pitt-Kethley

The Lady's Dressing-Room

Five hours (and who can do it less in?)
By haughty Celia spent in dressing;
The goddess from her chamber issues,
Arrayed in lace, brocade and tissues:
Strephon, who found the room was void,
And Betty, otherwise employed,
Stole in, and took a strict survey
Of all the litter, as it lay,
Whereof, to make the matter clear,
An inventory follows here.

And first, a dirty smock appeared,
Beneath the armpits well besmeared;
Strephon, the rogue, displayed it wide,
And turned it round on every side;
In such a case, few words are best,
And Strephon bids us guess the rest;
But swears how damnably the men lie
In calling Celia sweet and cleanly.

Now listen, while he next produces
The various combs for various uses;
Filled up with dirt so closely fixed
No brush could force a way betwixt;
A paste of composition rare,
Sweat, dandruff, powder, lead and hair,
A forehead-cloth with oil upon 't,
To smooth the wrinkles on her front;
Here, alum-flour to stop the steams
Exhaled from sour, unsavoury streams;
There, night-gloves made of Tripsey's hide
Bequeathed by Tripsey when she died;
With puppy-water, Beauty's help,
Distilled from Tripsey's darling whelp,
Here gally-pots and vials placed,

Some filled with washes, some with paste;
Some with pomatums, paints and slops,
And ointments good for scabby chops.
Hard by a filthy basin stands,
Fouled with the scouring of her hands;
The basin takes whatever comes,
The scrapings from her teeth and gums,
A nasty compound of all hues,
For here she spits, and here she spews.

But O! it turned poor Strephon's bowels
When he beheld and smelt the towels;
Begummed, besmattered and beslimed;
With dirt and sweat and ear-wax grimed.
No object Strephon's eye escapes;
Here petticoats in frowsy heaps.
Nor be the handkerchiefs forgot,
All varnished o'er with snuff and snot.
The stockings, why should I expose,
Stained with the moisture of her toes;
Of greasy coifs and pinners reeking,
Which Celia slept at least a week in.
A pair of tweezers next he found,
To pluck her brows in arches round,
Or hairs that sink the forehead low
Or, on her chin, like bristles grow.

The virtues we must not let pass
Of Celia's magnifying glass;
When frighted Strephon cast his eye on't
It showed the visage of a giant:
A glass that can to sight disclose
The smallest worm in Celia's nose,
And faithfully direct her nail
To squeeze it out from head to tail;
For, catch it nicely by the head,
It must come out, alive or dead.

Why, Strephon, will you tell the rest?
And must you needs describe the chest?
That careless wench! No creature warn her
To move it out from yonder corner,
But leave it standing full in sight
For you to exercise your spite!
In vain the workman showed his wit,
With rings and hinges counterfeit
To make it seem, in this disguise,
A cabinet to vulgar eyes;
Which Strephon ventured to look in,
Resolved to go through thick and thin,
He lifts the lid; there need no more,
He smelt it all the time before.

As, from within Pandora's box,
When Epimetheus op'd the locks,
A sudden universal crew
Of human evils upward flew;
He still was comforted to find
That Hope at last remained behind.

So, Strephon, lifting up the lid,
To view what in the chest was hid,
The vapours flew from out the vent;
But Strephon, cautious, never meant
The bottom of the pan to grope
And foul his hands in search of hope.

O! ne'er may such a vile machine
Be once in Celia's chamber seen!
O! may she better learn to keep
Those secrets of the hoary deep!

As mutton-cutlets, prime of meat,
Which, though with art you salt and beat
As laws of cookery require,
And roast them at the clearest fire;

If, from adown the hopeful chops,
The fat upon a cinder drops,
To stinking smoke it turns the flame,
Poisoning the flesh from whence it came,
And up exhales a greasy stench
For which you cursed the careless wench:
So, things which must not be expressed
When plumped into the reeking chest
Send up an excremental smell
To taint the parts from whence they fell:
The petticoats and gown perfume
And waft a stink round every room.

Thus, finishing his grand survey,
The swain, disgusted, slunk away,
Repeating, in his amorous fits,
Oh! Celia, Celia, Celia shits.

But Vengeance, goddess never sleeping,
Soon punished Strephon for his peeping.
His foul imagination links
Each dame he sees with all her stinks;
And if unsavoury odours fly,
Conceives a lady standing by.
All women his description fits
And both ideas jump like wits
By vicious fancy coupled fast
And still appearing in contrast.

I pity wretched Strephon, blind
To all the charms of womankind.
Should I the Queen of Love refuse
Because she rose from stinking ooze?
To him that looks behind the scene
Satira's but some pocky quean.

When Celia all her glory shows,
If Strephon will but stop his nose,
Who now so impiously blasphemes
Her ointments, daubs and paints and creams,
Her washes, slops and every clout
With which he makes so foul a rout,
He soon would learn to think like me,
And bless his ravished eyes to see
Such order from confusion sprung,
Such gaudy tulips raised from dung.

JONATHAN SWIFT

The Reasons That Induced Dr Swift to Write a Poem Called 'The Lady's Dressing-Room'

The Doctor in a clean, starched band,
His golden snuff-box in his hand,
With care his diamond ring displays
And artful shows his various rays,
While grave he stalks down — — Street
His dearest Betty — to meet.

Long had he waited for this hour,
Nor gained admittance to the bower,
Had joked and punned and swore and writ,
Tried all his gallantry and wit,
Had told her oft what part he bore
In Oxford's schemes in days of yore,
But bawdy, politics, nor satire
Could move this dull, hard-hearted creature.
Jenny, her maid, could taste a rhyme,
And grieved to see him lose his time,
Had kindly whispered in his ear,
For twice two pounds you enter here.
My lady vows, without that sum
It is in vain you write or come.

The destined offering now he brought
And in a paradise of thought,
With a low bow approached the dame
Who smiling heard him preach his flame.
His gold she takes (such proofs as these
Convince most unbelieving shes),
And in her trunk rose up to lock it
(Too wise to trust it to her pocket),
And then, returned with blushing grace,
Expects the Doctor's warm embrace.

But now this is the proper place
Where morals stare me in the face,
And, for the sake of fine expression,
I'm forced to make a small digression.
Alas for wretched humankind,
With learning mad, with wisdom blind!
The ox thinks he's for saddle fit
(As, long ago, friend Horace writ),
And men, their talents still mistaking,
The stutterer fancies his is speaking.
With admiration oft we see
Hard features heightened by toupee,
The beau affects the politician,
Wit is the citizen's ambition,
Poor Pope philosophy displays on
With so much rhyme and little reason,
And, though he argues ne'er so long
That all is right, his head is wrong.

None strive to know their proper merit
But strain for wisdom, beauty, spirit,
And lose the praise that is their due
While they've th' impossible in view.
So have I seen th' injudicious heir
To add one window th' whole house impair.

Instinct the hound does better teach,
Who never undertook to preach.
The frighted hare from dogs does run
But not attempts to bear a gun.
Here many noble thoughts occur,
But I prolixity abhor,
And will pursue th' instructive tale
To show the wise in some things fail.

The reverend lover with surprise
Peeps in her bubbies and her eyes,

And kisses both, and tries – and tries.
The evening in this hellish play,
Beside his guineas thrown away,
Provoked the priest to that degree
He swore, *The fault is not in me.*
Your damned close stool so near my nose,
Your dirty smock and stinking toes,
Would make a Hercules as tame
As any beau that you can name.

The nymph, grown furious, roared, *By God*
The blame lies all in sixty odd,
And, scornful, pointing to the door
Cried, *Fumbler, see my face no more*

With all my heart I'll go away
But, nothing done, I'll nothing pay.
Give back the money.

             How? cried she,
Would you palm such a cheat on me?
For poor four pound to roar and bellow,
Why sure you want some new prunella.
What if your verses have not sold,
Must I therefore return your gold?
Perhaps you have no better luck in
The knack of rhyming than of fucking.
I won't give back one single crown
To wash your band or turn your gown.

I'll be revenged, you saucy quean,
Replies the disappointed Dean.
I'll so describe your dressing-room.

She answered short, *I'm glad you'll write.*
You'll furnish paper when I shite.

LADY MARY WORTLEY MONTAGU

What'mmmIdoin'?

What'mmmIdoin'? slurs Lyris, feigning shock.
I'll tell you what you're doing: YOU
are doing what you always do,
even when you're sober SUCKING COCK!

MARTIAL
translated by Tony Harrison

I'm Placing in Your Hands My Lover and Myself

I'm placing in your hands my lover and myself,
Aurelius. A modest favour's all I'm after:
if something pretty untouched and innocent
has ever been your heart's desire, then keep
this young boy pure and safe for me – unchased!
Not safe from them outdoors: we've really got
no cause to fear the passers-by, deep in
their own affairs. It's you and that great prick
that frighten me: it's such a menace to
the nicest and the dirtiest boys alike.
Outside the house, feel free – you stick it in
just where and when and who and how you like.
But hands off this one! Fair enough, OK?
I know you're a shit with a nasty mind, so if
your ungovernable lust drives you to such
a pitch you try to pester him with dirty
tricks, I've got a fate lined up for you
far worse than death, you vicious bastard: dragged
out through the open door by the heels, you'll find
a radish bunch, a spiny mullet, jammed
straight up your arse'll split you cheek from cheek.

CATULLUS
translated by Rodney Pybus

The Temperaments

Nine adulteries, 12 liaisons, 64 fornications and something
    approaching a rape
Rest nightly upon the soul of our dear friend Florialis,
And yet the man is so quiet and reserved in demeanour
That he passes for both bloodless and sexless.
Bastidides, on the contrary, who both talks and writes of
    nothing save copulation,
Has become the father of twins,
But he accomplished the feat at some cost;
He had to be four times cuckolded.

EZRA POUND

PARTS OF THE BODY,
MOSTLY MALE

The Young Lady of Exeter

There was a young lady of Exeter
So pretty that men craned their necks at her,
    And one went so far
    As to wave from his car
The distinguishing mark of his sex at her.

ANON.

The Fifth Column

The Fifth Column
between my legs,
the mauve toad
with hairy eggs,
garlic sausage
with an appetite,
my magic wand
of dynamite,
has this minute
commissioned me
to write his auto-
biography.

DUNCAN FORBES

I Am Not Made of Fragile Elm

I am not made of fragile elm
and though I wear a fluted helm
I always stand with rigid shaft
however deep or fierce the draught!
My sappy life is given dress
in carvings of long-lived cypress —
a thousand days within my sight
are one tired moon and one bright night,
and like the rose that roots in clay
I live to shoot another day.
Then all who come here out of bounds,
be warned that these are sacred grounds,
just lay a hand on plant or house
and I who guard as well as rouse
will punish the offender where
my kingdom stops by half a hair.
Take note, I am Priapus who
engenders love and virtue too;
my punishments in clusters come,
I plant ripe figs inside your bum
and every thief who jails avoids
shall bear my crop of haemorrhoids.

MARTIAL
translated by Peter Porter

The Self-Exposed

On the Bangor-bound platform, the crowd became one
Shaping lips to me: *Now, sweet now! –*
On the handle of my zipper, my hand dragged down,
Out it budded, my golden bough

In that plate-glass proscenium my Pullman room.
An old biddy guffawed, a valise
Being handed up to a conductor's hand
Blossomed underwear, a man yelled *Police! –*

Then we lurched, I was gone. What gets into me?
I'm not one to be peter-proud,
But my bird-out-of-hand longs to take its stand
On the farther side from what's allowed.

People with their foreheads like income tax forms
Raise the puke in me! How I yearn
To scribble with my dibble on their neat-ruled norms.
They'll nail me yet. I never learn.

Oh, I've been to psychiatrist and priest,
I've read an uplifting book,
But it's cold, and I hunger to walk forth dressed
In the quilt of the world's warm look.

X. J. KENNEDY

Nocturne

I see the local satyr stand
at night in foliage on the wall
surprised I take another look
the thing's still flaccid in his hand

As self-exposed as unfulfilled
my longing stands between these leaves
risible, grievous to itself
it knows what can – cannot – be willed

For Love the great phenomenon
that saw my too immodest hope
has touched my breast and said goodbye
and turned the corner and is gone

GERDA MAYER

The Poet Holds His Future in His Hand

Tonight I looked at it; I don't often

it performs its two functions well enough
in return I keep it reasonably clean

but quite by chance I looked at it tonight
and there were several dirty marks on it

I of course looked harder: and they were veins
underneath the skin, bloody great black veins!

they weren't there last time I happened to look
certainly the light was bad in that place

but there's no doubt that the pressure is on

B. S. JOHNSON

Politics of Envy

In the Jackdaw folder of 'Historical Genitalia',
The suitors of Elizabeth and reasons for their failure,
The Bonsai quality of Buonaparte's regalia,
What Hitler was missing in the region of Westphalia
Would all be investigated *inter* many *alia*.

Elizabeth I in a miniature by Hilliard
Scanned for masculinity by Hotson, Rowse and Tillyard,
The gusset of Napoleon expounded like the *Iliad*,
Hitler in his bunker playing pocket billiard
Would all be reproduced by the chiliad or milliard.

But if the young princess's *pudenda* were like Alice's
And only redetermined by Elizabethan malices,
If Buonaparte's was small because he owned huge palaces
And Hitler lost a ball when he gave the globe paralysis,
Do malicious jealousies provide all phallic fallacies?

DUNCAN FORBES

Connoisseur

I love the ballet.
As I watch them plié
I keep wondering who's gay,
But by oath,
I could simply not say if
Dear Rudi Nureyev
Is AC or DC
Or both.

As he leaps through the air
With his taut derrière,
His thighs engineered
Like an ox.
His nostrils aflare . . .
I think I know where
He conveniently keeps
His old socks.

JOAN VAN POZNAK

Clown's Song

When that I was and a little tiny boy,
   With hey, ho, the wind and the rain,
A foolish thing was but a toy,
   For the rain it raineth every day.

But when I came to man's estate,
   With hey, ho, the wind and the rain,
'Gainst knaves and thieves men shut their gate,
   For the rain it raineth every day.

But when I came, alas, to wive,
   With hey, ho, the wind and the rain,
By swaggering could I never thrive,
   For the rain it raineth every day.

But when I came unto my beds,
   With hey, ho, the wind and the rain,
With tosspots still had drunken heads,
   For the rain it raineth every day.

A great while ago the world begun,
   With hey, ho, the wind and the rain;
But that's all one, our play is done,
   And we'll strive to please you every day.

WILLIAM SHAKESPEARE

A Person Is Accidentally Rejuvenated in Old Age

When a cat flea bit my scrotum
my cock shot up like a totem pole;
I was near to death's dark portal,
but that flea roused my immortal soul!

And I had no heart to kill it,
it restored my lost virility!
It's a fact, to be quite truthful,
I was born again! A youthful me!

Spirits of delight come rarely,
things like that are always fairly few;
angels in the world of men, they
cause ecstatic feelings when they do!

GAVIN EWART

Down, Wanton, Down!

Down, wanton, down! Have you no shame
That at the whisper of Love's name,
Or Beauty's, presto! up you raise
Your angry head and stand at gaze?

Poor Bombard-captain, sworn to reach
The ravelin and effect a breach —
Indifferent what you storm or why,
So be that in the breach you die!

Love may be blind, but Love at least
Knows what is man and what mere beast;
Or Beauty wayward, but requires
More delicacy from her squires.

Tell me, my witless, whose one boast
Could be your staunchness at the post,
When were you made a man of parts
To think fine and profess the arts?

Will many-gifted Beauty come
Bowing to your bald rule of thumb,
Or Love swear loyalty to your crown?
Be gone, have done! Down, wanton, down!

ROBERT GRAVES

Those Upright Men

I heard of a tribe where the men
                held their erections all their lives,
like rhino horns: each
his own mascot before the main regiment of the body,
gorgeous trophies
                painful to bump.

How was it done? by jockstraps
                    loincloths de luxe
with withies?
          by suggestion?
the curves of their own country as they hunted,
the round waterhole, the swollenness of coconuts
the plump streams
              coiling and juicing from the buttocks
              of herbaceous mountains?

Were their dreams never dry?
              love men of endless fervor
or were they the red-eyed servants of their women,
hot and cold for endless foreplay?
or were they workers, exploited, forklifting their semen
              under stern state frottage,
for there were few men in their nation:
                  in numbers not large.

Or was it just   virilismus
          a muscular kink?

They painted themselves, for ceremonial
in colour contrasts of rising bands of pigments
                  of riverbank clay
        red, white and blue.

Those upright men
I believe, wore their cocks instead of ties
or truths
or guns;

or socks.

JUDITH KAZANTZIS

Lady Lowbodice

Every time Lady Lowbodice swoons
Her bubbies pop out like balloons,
    But her butler stands by
    With hauteur in his eye
And lifts them back in with warm spoons.

ANON.

Anointed Vessel

Admire the watered silky gap,
Mahomet's paradise, that shows
My creamy entry through the lap
Of luxuries that once were rose.

Oh, tired old eyes, take up delight
As painters do, forget your tears
Though warranted, in this rich sight –
This vessel that uplifts and cheers:

In a soft box of plushy fluff,
Black, but with glints of copper-red
And edges crinkly like a ruff,
Lies the great god of gems in bed,

Throbbing with sap and life, and sends
In wafts the best news ever sent,
A perfume his ecstatic friends
Think stolen from each element.

But contemplate this temple cont-
emplate, then get your breath, and kiss
The jewel having fits in front,
The ruby grinning for its bliss,

Flower of the inner court, kid brother
So mad about the taller one
It kisses till they both half-smother
And puff, then pulse, in unison . . .

But rest; you're blazing now; relax.
It too should calm and cool; but rest? –
In those embrasures and hot cracks
Of thigh and belly, breast and breast?

No, soon its swaying tipsiness
Wins my parts over to a man.
My flesh stands up and nods: right dress!
Begin again where we began!

PAUL VERLAINE
translated by Alistair Elliot

Arsehole

It is shy as a gathered eyelet
neatly worked in shrinking violet;
it is the dilating iris, tucked
away, a tightening throb when fucked.

It is a soiled and puckered hem,
the golden treasury's privy purse.
With all the colours of a bruise,
it is the fleck of blood in albumen.

I dreamed your body was an instrument
and this was the worn mouthpiece
to which my breathing lips were bent.

Each note pleaded to love a little longer,
longer, as though it was dying of hunger.
I fed that famished mouth my ambergris.

CRAIG RAINE

Lines on the Arsehole: A Sonnet

Crumpled like a carnation, mauve and dim
It breathes, cowering humbly in the moss
Still wet with love which trickles down across
The soft slope of white buttocks to its rim.

Threads like long tears of milk blown radiantly
Out by the cruel gust that turns them back
Weep home again along the cambered track
Through reddish clinkers and wild bilberry.

My mouth mates often with this breathing-hole.
While matter goes and comes, my jealous soul
Makes tawny tears there in its nest of sighs:

This olive is a swoon, this flute whose stop
Teases the tube where heaven's soft-centres drop,
This female Promised Land where warm springs rise.

PAUL VERLAINE (OCTET) AND ARTHUR RIMBAUD (SESTET)
translated by Alistair Elliot

The Sexual Sigh

The small buttocks of men, that excite the women . . .
but ah! the beautiful feminine broadness!

GAVIN EWART

GETTING RELIGION

Haiku: The Wisdom of the Streets

God is a flasher.
He reveals himself to some,
but not to others.

GAVIN EWART

The Penurious Quaker *or*
The High Priz'd Harlot

Quaker. My Friend thy Beauty seemeth good
    We Righteous have our failings;
I'm Flesh and Blood, methinks I cou'd,
    Wert thou but free from Ailings.

Harlot. Believe me Sir I'm newly broach'd,
    And never have been in yet;
I vow and swear I ne'er was touch'd,
    By Man 'till this day sennight.

Quaker. Then prithee Friend, now prithee do,
    Nay, let us not defer it;
And I'll be kind to thee when thou
    Hast laid the Evil Spirit.

Harlot. I vow I won't, indeed I shan't,
    Unless I've Money first, Sir;
For if I ever trust a Saint,
    I wish I may be curst, Sir.

Quaker. I cannot like the Wicked say,
    I Love thee and Adore thee,
And therefore thou wilt make me pay,
    So here is Six pence for thee.

Harlot. Confound you for a stingy *Whig*,
    Do ye think I live by Stealing;
Farewel you Puritannick Prig,
    I scorn to take your Shilling.

ANON.

from Some More Cases of Love with Solutions

I

Q: At the Jesuits' church, the sexton father's racked
    With lust; and keen to keep his lust in order
    He dips his balls and prick in holy water.
    Now is that sacrilege or a holy act?

A: The sexton father should be praised indeed
    If dipping balls and prick in holy water
    He kept his swingeing lechery in order,
    Staying free and easy from the sins of seed.

II

Q: The abbess woke up frantic after she
    Had dreamed all night of eating gooseberry fool,
    To find her mouth full of the abbot's tool.
    How had she sinned, though? Greed? Or lechery?

A: She didn't sin, as far as we make out,
    In either way. It was an accident –
    Although, if she had found it in her cunt
    Or up her arse, there might have been some doubt.

III

Q: Sister Prue, to relieve a bout of nerves
    Which blocked the flow of holy orisons,
    Had herself screwed by two fat friars at once.
    The question is, what penance she deserves.

A: If it was just to let her prayers out
    She had them penetrate her to the hilt,
    She needn't feel the smallest prick of guilt:
    There is no penance laid on the devout.

IV

Q: Brother Albert, in the heat of the dog-days,
   Tossed off his novices to save their skins
   From idleness and its adjacent sins.
   Was this too worldly to deserve our praise?

A: Temptation always rules the idle will,
   So, good for him, if Albert tossed their midget
   Organs off; and if he'd fucked them rigid,
   That should be counted more heroic still.

ATTRIBUTED TO PIETRO ARETINO
translated by Alistair Elliot

Godly Girzie

The night it was a holy night,
   The day had been a holy day;
Kilmarnock gleam'd wi' candle light,
   As Girzie hameward took her way.
A man o' sin, ill may he thrive!
   And never holy meeting see!
With godly Girzie met belyve,
   Amang the Craigie hills sae hie.

The chiel' was wight, the chiel' was stark
   He wad na wait to chap nor ca'
And she was faint wi' holy wark,
   She had na pith to say him na.
But ay she glowr'd up to the moon,
   And ay she sigh'd most piouslie,
'I trust my heart's in heaven aboon,
   'Whare'er your sinfu' pintle be.'

ROBERT BURNS

Holy Willie's Prayer

And send the godly in a pet to pray. Pope

O Thou that in the Heavens does dwell,
Wha, as it pleases best Thysel,
Sends ane to Heaven an' ten to Hell
    A' for thy glory,
And no for onie gude or ill
    They've done before Thee!

I bless and praise Thy matchless might,
When thousands Thou has left in night,
That I am here before Thy sight
    For gifts an' grace
A burning and a shining light
    To a' this place.

What was I, or my generation,
That I should get sic exaltation?
I, wha deserv'd most just damnation
    For broken laws
Sax thousand years ere my creation,
    Thro' Adam's cause!

When from my mither's womb I fell,
Thou might hae plung'd me deep in hell
To gnash my gooms, and weep, and wail
    In burning lakes,
Where damned devils roar and yell,
    Chain'd to their stakes.

Yet I am here, a chosen sample,
To show Thy grace is great and ample:
I'm here a pillar o' Thy temple,
    Strong as a rock,
A guide, a buckler, and example
    To a' Thy flock!

But yet, O Lord! confess I must:
At times I'm fash'd wi' fleshly lust;
An' sometimes, too, in warldly trust
    Vile self gets in;
But Thou remembers we are dust,
    Defiled wi' sin.

O Lord! yestreen, Thou kens, wi' Meg —
Thy pardon I sincerely beg —
O' may't ne'er be a living plague
    To my dishonour!
An' I'll ne'er lift a lawless leg
    Again upon her.

Besides, I farther maun avow —
Wi' Leezie's lass, three times, I trow —
But, Lord, that Friday I was fou,
    When I cam near her,
Or else, Thou kens, Thy servant true
    Wad never steer her.

Maybe Thou lets this fleshly thorn
Buffet Thy servant e'en and morn,
Lest he owre-proud and high should turn
    That he's sae gifted:
If sae, Thy han' maun e'en be borne
    Until Thou lift it.

Lord, bless Thy chosen in this place,
For here Thou has a chosen race!
But God confound their stubborn face
    An' blast their name,
Wha brings Thy elders to disgrace
    An' open shame!

Lord, mind Gau'n Hamilton's deserts:
He drinks, an' swears, an' plays at cartes,
Yet has sae monie takin arts
    Wi' great and sma',

Frae God's ain Priest the people's hearts
    He steals awa.

And when we chasten'd him therefore,
Thou kens how he bred sic a splore,
And set the warld in a roar
    O' laughin at us:
Curse Thou his basket and his store,
    Kail an' potatoes!

Lord, hear my earnest cry and pray'r
Against that Presbyt'ry of Ayr!
Thy strong right hand, Lord, make it bare
    Upo' their heads!
Lord, visit them, an' dinna spare
    For their misdeeds!

O Lord, my God! that glib-tongu'd Aiken,
My vera heart and flesh are quakin
To think how we stood sweatin, shakin,
    An' pish'd wi' dread,
While Auld, wi' hingin lip gaed sneaking
    And hid his head.

Lord, in Thy day o' veangeance try him!
Lord, visit him wha did employ him!
And pass not in Thy mercy by them
    Nor hear their pray'r,
But for Thy people's sake destroy them,
    An' dinna spare!

But Lord, remember me and mine
Wi' mercies temporal and divine,
That I for grace an' gear may shine
    Excell'd by nane;
And a' the glory shall be Thine –
    Amen, Amen!

ROBERT BURNS

The Presbyterian Wedding

A certain Presbyterian Pair
   Were wedded t'other day;
And when in Bed the Lambs were laid,
   Their Pastor came to pray.

But first he bade each Guest depart,
   Nor sacred Rites prophane;
For carnal Eyes such Mysteries
   Can never entertain.

Then with a puritannick Air,
   Unto the Lord he pray'd,
That he would please to grant Encrease
   To that same man and maid:

And that the Husbandman might dress
   Full well the Vine his Wife;
And like a Vine she still might twine
   About him all her Life.

Sack posset then he gave them both,
   And said with lifted Eyes,
Blest of the Lord! with one Accord
   Begin your Enterprize.

The Bridgroom then drew near his Spouse,
   T'apply Prolifick Balm;
And while they strove in mutual Love,
   The Parson sung a Psalm.

ANON.

The Size of the Mother Superior

The size of the Mother Superior
Made a tongue-job as weary, nay wearier
    Than late Henry James,
    The Commonwealth Games,
Or an evening of *opera seria*.

JOHN FULLER AND JAMES FENTON

from Bulsh
In memoriam Alfred Jarry

Bulsh in the desert prays, and camels bawl:
'Head for the hills before he humps us all!'

If visions of delight goad Bulsh, he'll beat
His breast, and if they goad him twice, his meat.

Plump girls stay pasted fast to Bulsh's slat,
Old bony ones he shrives in no time flat.

Wise nuns at Mass keep bulldogs in their pew
Lest Bulsh's fingers play the Wandering Jew.

Young matrons pray, 'Saint Bulsh, man, get me pregnant!'
(His device: testicles, with penis regnant.)

Satan
I'll net the big trout yet. One of my ploys
Is dangling Bulsh pink wriggling altar boys.

Bulsh's carpe diem
Almighty God's a patient elevator.
Drink and fuck now, and be assumpted later.

X. J. KENNEDY

A Morningside Lady

A Morningside Lady named Alice
Once pissed in the Catholic chalice.
    Alas! 'Twas not need
    That occasioned the deed
But pure Presbyterian malice.

ANON.

Heaven: Behind Closed Doors

The necessary despairing cry of
Great Men everywhere: Hello and goodbye.

'What?' Mary gasps. 'Away *again . . . tonight?*'

God, helpless leader, displays empty palms.
'It's the Newsletter editorial.
For all those who can't see me face to face.
So many can't.'

                'You can say *that* again,'
Mary says, to her imaginary friend.

'Look,' he pleads. 'I'll get away, we'll have a
Few drinks.' Voice low now – and hoarse. 'You could slip
Into one of those outfits . . . like you said.'

'And me thinking you liked white,' Mary sighs.

God palms his ancient brow in disbelief.
An eternity of misunderstanding
Can weary even the gladdest heart.
'I *love* you in white. We all know you suit
White. It's just . . . sometimes I'd like a *change.*'

'Admit it – you've always been bored with white.'

'No! You're a marvellous Queen of Heaven.
Don't get me wrong.' As though holding in cupped
Hands a new and incredibly delicate
Species, God drops his voice to a whisper.
'It's just you're so . . . *passive* sometimes. You don't
Do anything.' He should stop – but the words
Burst out. 'I'd love you to *sit on my face.*'

No repulsive insect dropped on bare skin
Could have caused Mary such disgust and pain.
'You *created* me,' she howls, 'and got your
Virgin bride and mother all in white, your
Exemplar and icon, great at PR.
If you want your face sat on *make a whore.*'

'I don't want a whore,' God shouts. 'I want *you*
To sit on me – *you* . . . of your own free will.
That's what free will's for. The parameters
Only look fixed. They can all be changed.'

'I tried – but it's not me,' Mary objects.

'Massage the parameters!' God fiercely
Cries, moulding air with a sculptor's caress,
His face bright with the passion and love that
Shaped Man in the sixth dawn. Not today though.
There is nothing before him but empty air.
The fervour fades slowly, the hands grow still.

Each is silent, lost in a private dream.

'And I thought you enjoyed it,' Mary grieves.

'Massage them,' God helplessly, feebly sighs.

Mary's grumpy last shot: '*Massage your own.*'

MICHAEL FOLEY

From the Depths of the Crypt

From the depths of the crypt at St Giles
Came a scream that resounded for miles.
    Said the vicar, 'Good gracious!
    Has Father Ignatius
Forgotten the Bishop has piles?'

        ANON.

LAST WORDS

As the Poets Have Mournfully Sung

As the poets have mournfully sung,
Death takes the innocent young,
    The rolling in money,
    The screamingly funny,
And those who are very well hung.

W. H. AUDEN

Epitaph on Pegasus, a Limping Gay

Oh, passer-by, should you inquire
About my name or my desire
Then know that buried 'neath this sod
Halt Pegasus awaits his God.
Learn his request now you've his name
And then you'll satisfy the same:
Whene'er a willing boy you'd lay,
Oh, screw him on my tomb, I pray.
'Tis not incense but coition
Eases souls in their perdition,
Such requiems a ghost desires
As sweetest respite 'midst Hell's fires.
Our ancestors on this truth seized:
Achilles Chiron's ghost appeased
When blond Patroclus' bottom knew
The pleasures of a well-wrought screw,
While Hercules first pierced his lad
When at the fun'ral of his dad.
So, like the ancients, I advise
You too should make this sacrifice.

ANTONIO BECCADELLI
translated by Stephen Coote

Annus Miserabilis

Yes, sexual intercourse began
   In nineteen sixty-three,
But didn't satisfy my man
   For very long – nor me.

Four-seater frolics in the Jag,
   The weekends spent wife-swopping.
I'd buy the latest contact mag
   When I did the shopping.

'Couple, AC/DC, seeks
   Similar for fun;
Discretion guaranteed – no freaks.'
   We answered every one.

We met a lot of folk that way:
   Long-stayers, well-endowed.
We weren't choosy, straight or gay,
   Three never made a crowd.

But You-Know-What blew that sky-high;
   No point in tempting fate.
Now we're strictly DIY
   In nineteen eighty-eight.

SIMON RAE

Smokers for Celibacy

Some of us are a little tired of hearing that cigarettes kill.
We'd like to warn you about another way of making
  yourself ill:

we suggest that in view of AIDS, herpes, chlamydia, cystitis
  and NSU,
not to mention genital warts and cervical cancer and the
  proven connection between the two,

if you want to avoid turning into physical wrecks
what you should give up is not smoking but sex.

We're sorry if you're upset,
but think of the grisly things you might otherwise get.

We can't see much point in avoiding emphysema at sixty-
  five
if that's an age at which you have conspicuously failed to
  arrive,

and as for cancer, it is a depressing fact
that at least for women this disease is more likely to occur
  in the reproductive tract.

We could name friends of ours who died that way, if you
  insist,
but we feel sure you can each provide your own list.

You'll notice we didn't mention syphilis and gonorrhoea;
well, we have now, so don't get the idea

that, just because of antibiotics, quaint old clap and pox
are not still being generously spread around by men's cocks.

Some of us aren't too keen on the thought of micro-
  organisms travelling up into our brain
and giving us General Paralysis of the Insane.

We're opting out of one-night stands:
we'd rather have a cigarette in our hands.

[284]

If it's a choice between two objects of cylindrical shape
we go for the one that is seldom if ever guilty of rape.

Cigarettes just lie there quietly in their packs
waiting until you call on one of them to help you relax.

They aren't moody: they don't go in for sexual harassment
    and threats,
or worry about their performance as compared with that of
    other cigarettes,

nor do they keep you awake all night telling you the story
    of their life,
beginning with their mother and going on until morning
    about their first wife.

Above all, the residues they leave in your system are
    thoroughly sterilized and clean,
which is more than can be said for the products of the
    human machine.

Altogether, we've come to the conclusion that sex is a drag.
Just give us a fag.

FLEUR ADCOCK

Fforestfawr

When they saw off Dai Evans's da
The whole thing was done very nice:
Bethesda was packed to the doors,
And the minister, Urien Price,
Addressed them with telling effect.

'Our brother grew rich in respect,'
He told them in accents of fire;
'A man of unshakeable strength,
Whom to know was at once to admire.
He did nothing common or mean.'

They'd no notion of coming between
That poor young Dai and his grief,
So each of them just had a word
With him after, well-chosen and brief:
'I looked up to him, boy' sort of touch.

He thanked one and all very much,
But thought, as he waved them goodbye,
Was respect going to be what they felt
When Bethesda did honour to Dai?
No, something more personal, see?

'Hallo, pet. Alone? Good. It's me.
Ah now, who did you think it was?
Well, come down the Bush and find out.
You'll know me easy, because
I'm wearing a black tie, love.'

KINGSLEY AMIS

The Book of the Law

The Lord deplored unwedded bliss
And so perfected syphilis.
If, after twenty years of screw,
Your nose drops off, it's balls to you.
And don't become a sodomite:
He'll give you AIDS, and serve you right
You filthy, fornicating beast.

You should have been a Catholic priest.

JOHN WHITWORTH

EVERYONE SANG

The Ball of Kirriemuir

According to James Barke (*Pornography and Bawdry in Literature and Society*, Glasgow, 1958) the original ballad celebrated an actual event in the 1880s. When the Highland Division paraded before Churchill in Tripoli after the successful North Africa campaign this is what they were singing. Churchill 'grinned broadly' but the BBC recording was not broadcast. It has been so embroidered and enlarged over the last hundred years that it is no longer particularly Scots, has no beginning and no end, and is known in part, at least the chorus (not original, according to Barke), to almost everybody. What follows is a quite undefinitive selection.

Four and twenty virgins
Came down from Inverness,
But when the ball was over
There were four and twenty less,

Singing balls to your partner,
Arses to the wall.
If you've never been fucked on a Saturday night
You've never been fucked at all.

There was fucking in the hayloft;
There was fucking in the ricks.
Why, you'd scarcely hear the music for
The swishing of the pricks,

Singing etc.

The Minister was there of course
And started with a hymn.
He knelt and prayed with every maid
Before he filled her quim,

Singing etc.

The elders of the Kirk were there,
All scandalized to see
Four and twenty maidenheads
A-hanging on a tree,

Singing etc.

The lady organist was there,
All buckled to the front,
A wreath of roses round her arse
And thistles round her cunt,

Singing etc.

The undertaker he was there.
He wore a long black shroud
And perched upon the mantelpiece
To wank into the crowd,

Singing etc.

They were sucking in the parlour;
They were screwing on the stairs.
The piper swore the dancing floor
Was black with pubic hairs,

Singing etc.

The village butcher he was there,
His cleaver in his hand.
He danced a reel and flashed his steel
And circumcised the band,

Singing etc.

The fishmonger was there as well,
A stinking, slippery sod.
He used his hand but couldn't stand
And had to use a cod,

Singing etc.

The village cripple he was there
But wasn't up to much.
He tripped them with his wooden leg
Then stuffed them with his crutch,

Singing etc.

The conjurer was there as well
And worked a clever trick.
He pulled his foreskin over his head
And vanished up his prick,

Singing etc.

The schoolmaster was there, of course
And screwed by rule of thumb,
By logarithms working out
The time that he would come,

Singing etc.

The Lady of the Manor, she
Had kept us all in fits
By swinging from the chandelier
And sliding on her tits,

Singing etc.

They fucked them on the balcony;
They fucked them in the hall.
God save us, said the porter, *but
They've come to fuck us all,*

Singing etc.

Up in the morning early, and
The farmer nearly shat,
For forty acres of his corn
Was fairly fuckit flat,

Singing etc.

So when the ball was over, then
The maidens all confessed
That while they liked the music fine
The fucking was the best,

Singing etc.

ANON.

Acknowledgements

We are indebted to the copyright holders for permission to reprint certain poems:

FLEUR ADCOCK: from *Selected Poems* (1983), reprinted by permission of Oxford University Press; from *The Catalogue* (1987), reprinted by permission of Bloodaxe Books Ltd; KINGSLEY AMIS: from *Collected Poems 1944–79*, reprinted by permission of Random Century Ltd; W. H. AUDEN: from *Collected Poems*, reprinted by permission of Faber and Faber Ltd and Random House; SEBASTIAN BARKER: from *On The Rocks*, reprinted by permission of Martin Brian & O'Keeffe Ltd; ELIZABETH BARTLETT: from *The Czar Is Dead* (Rivelin Grapheme Press), reprinted by permission of the author; JOHN BERRYMAN: from *77 Dream Songs*, reprinted by permission of Faber and Faber Ltd and Farrar, Straus & Giroux Inc.; ALAN BOLD: 'A Special Theory of Relativity', by permission of the author; C. P. CAVAFY: from *Collected Poems* translated by Edmund Keeley and Philip Sherrard, reprinted by permission of the Estate of C. P. Cavafy, the translators and Chatto & Windus/The Hogarth Press; STEPHEN COOTE: from *The Penguin Book of Homosexual Verse*, reprinted by permission of Penguin Books Ltd and the author; WENDY COPE: from *Making Cocoa for Kingsley Amis*, reprinted by permission of Faber and Faber Ltd; ROGER CRAWFORD: 'The Love Song of Tommo Frogley' reprinted by permission of the author; e. e. cummings: from *Selected Poems 1923–1958*, reprinted by permission of Grafton Books and Liveright Publishing; J. V. CUNNINGHAM: from *Collected Poems and Epigrams*, reprinted with the permission of The Ohio University Press, Athens; CAROL ANN DUFFY: from *Standing Female Nude*, reprinted by permission of Anvil Press Poetry Ltd; LAWRENCE DURRELL: from *Collected Poems 1935–1963*, reprinted by permission of Faber and Faber Ltd and Curtis Brown Ltd; GAVIN EWART: from *The Collected Ewart* and *The New Ewart*, reprinted by permission of Random Century Ltd; other poems by permission of the author; T. S. ELIOT: 'Columbiad: Two Stanzos', 'There was a young girl of Siberia', and ''Twas Christmas on the Spanish Main', reprinted by kind permission of Mrs Valerie Eliot and SET; ALISTAIR ELLIOT: from *Femmes/Hombres*, reprinted by permission of Anvil Press Poetry Ltd; other poems by permission of the author; ZOË FAIRBAIRNS: from *One Foot on the Mountain*, Ed. Lilian Mohin, reprinted by permission of Onlywomen Press Ltd and the author; JAMES FENTON and JOHN FULLER: from *Partingtime Hall* (Viking Penguin), reprinted by permission of the Peters Fraser & Dunlop Group Ltd; MICHAEL FOLEY: 'Heaven Behind Closed Doors', reprinted by permission of the author; DUNCAN FORBES: from *August Autumn* (Secker & Warburg), reprinted by permission of the author; OLIVER ST JOHN GOGARTY: from *Oliver St John Gogarty* by Ulick O'Connor, reprinted by permission of Doubleday Co. Inc.; ROBERT GRAVES: from *Collected Poems 1975*, reprinted by permission of A. P. Watt Ltd on behalf of The Trustees of the Robert Graves Copyright Trust and by Oxford University Press Inc. (New York); PAUL GROVES: two poems by permission of the author; THOM GUNN: from *The Passages of Joy*, reprinted by permission of Faber and Faber Ltd and Farrar, Straus & Giroux Inc.; BERNARD GUTTERIDGE: from *Old Damson Face*, reprinted by permission of London Magazine Editions; MARILYN HACKER: from *Love, Death and the Changing of the Seasons*, reprinted by permission of Onlywomen Press Ltd; TONY HARRISON: from *The Loiners*, reprinted by permission of London Magazine Editions; from *U.S. Martial*, reprinted by permission of Bloodaxe Books Ltd; SEAMUS HEANEY: from *Door into the Dark*, reprinted by permission of Faber and Faber Ltd and Farrar, Straus & Giroux Inc.; SELIMA HILL: from *Saying Hello at the Station*, reprinted by permission of Chatto & Windus/The Hogarth Press; HAMISH IMLACH: 'Cod-Liver Oil and the Orange Juice', printed by permission of Heathside Music and the author; B. S. JOHNSON: from *Poems*, reprinted by permission of Constable & Co. Ltd; SYLVIA KANTARIS: poem by permission of the author; JUDITH KAZANTZIS: from *The Wicked Queen*, reprinted by permission of Sidgwick & Jackson Ltd; X. J. KENNEDY: from *Breaking and Entering* (Oxford University Press), reprinted by permission of Curtis Brown Ltd, copyright Self-exposed © 1969, Bulsh © 1970, and A. P. Watt Ltd; LINCOLN KIRSTEIN: poem by permission of the author; JOHN LATHAM: poem by permission of the author; ROBERT MAITRE: three poems by permission of the author; GERDA MAYER: two poems by permission of the author; JAMES MICHIE: translation of Catullus reprinted by permission of the author; CHRISTOPHER MIDDLETON: from *Pataxanadu*, reprinted by permission of Carcanet Press Ltd; EDNA ST VINCENT MILLAY: from *Collected Poems*, reprinted by permission of Harper & Row, Publishers; EDWIN MORGAN: from *Poems of Thirty Years*, reprinted by permission of Carcanet Press Ltd; GRACE NICHOLS: from *Thoughts of a Lazy Woman*, reprinted by permission of Virago Press Ltd; PATRICK O'SHAUGHNESSY: poem reprinted by permission of the author; TOM PICKARD: from *High on the Walls*, reprinted by

permission of Fulcrum Press and the author; FERGUS PICKERING:
three translations by permission of the author; FIONA PITT-KETHLEY:
from *Epigrams of Martial Englished by Divers Hands*, copyright ©
1987 the Regents of the University of California, reprinted by
permission of the University of California Press; PETER PORTER: from
Collected Poems, reprinted by permission of Oxford University Press;
J. A. POTTS: from *Epigrams of Martial Englished by Divers Hands*,
copyright © 1987 the Regents of the University of California,
reprinted by permission of the University of California Press; EZRA
POUND: from *Collected Poems*, reprinted by permission of Faber and
Faber Ltd and New Directions Publishing Corporation; RODNEY
PYBUS: translations from Catullus, printed by permission of the
author; SIMON RAE: poems reprinted by permission of the author;
CRAIG RAINE: from *A Martian Sends a Postcard Home*, reprinted by
permission of Oxford University Press; from *Rich*, reprinted by
permission of Faber and Faber Ltd; PETER READING: from *Essential
Reading*, reprinted by permission of Martin Secker & Warburg; JOHN
ROBINSON: poem by permission of the author; WILLIAM SCAMMELL:
poem by permission of the author; CAMERON SELF: poem by
permission of the author; LAWRENCE SUTTON: poem by permission
of the author; CHARLES THOMSON: poem by permission of the
author; MIKE THURLOW: poem by permission of the author; JOAN
VAN POZNAK: poems by permission of the author; JOHN
WHITWORTH: from *Tennis & Sex & Death*, reprinted by permission
of Peterloo Poets; HUGO WILLIAMS: from *Self-Portrait (With a Slide)*,
reprinted by permission of Oxford University Press; KIT WRIGHT:
from *Poems 1974–1983*, reprinted by permission of Random Century
Ltd.

Faber and Faber Ltd apologizes for any errors or omissions in the
above list and would be grateful to be notified of any corrections that
should be incorporated in the next edition of this volume.

Index of Poets

Index of Titles

Index of First Lines